The Gasser Collection

From the
GASSER COLLECTION

Given by the friends of
WILLIAM D. GASSER, CPA

In honor of his being named
Professor
and
Outstanding Teacher for 1971
June 24, 1971

Wallace Memorial Library
Rochester Institute of Technology

Brand Assets

Brand Assets

Tony Tollington

JOHN WILEY & SONS, LTD

Other Wiley Editorial Offices

John Wiley & Sons, Inc., 605 Third Avenue,
New York, NY 10158-0012, USA

WILEY-VCH GmbH, Pappelallee 3,
D-69469 Weinheim, Germany

John Wiley & Sons Australia Ltd, 33 Park Road, Milton,
Queensland 4064, Australia

John Wiley & Sons (Asia) Pte Ltd, 2 Clementi Loop #02-01,
Jin Xing Distripark, Singapore 129809

John Wiley & Sons (Canada) Ltd, 22 Worcester Road,
Rexdale, Ontario M9W 1L1, Canada

British Library Cataloguing in Publication Data

A catalogue record for this book is available from the British Library

ISBN 0-470-84423-X

Typeset in 10/12pt Times Roman by Laserwords Private Limited, Chennai, India
Printed and bound in Great Britain by TJ International Ltd, Padstow, Cornwall
This book is printed on acid-free paper responsibly manufactured from sustainable forestation, for
which at least two trees are planted for each one used for paper production.

Contents

Foreword

Brand valuation companies advance the case for the greater disclosure of brand assets on the balance sheet based upon commercial realism. We do so because we believe that the real wealth creators in a business are often their intangible assets, in particular their brand assets. So, for example, we regard it as nonsensical that the accounting profession should distinguish between purchased brands and internally generated brands for capitalisation purposes.

An argument in support of commercial realism is that the need for relevant information is now more powerful than the need for reliable information. Let me explain. The accounting profession is driven by the need to produce *reliable* information using transaction-based values, which tends to restrict independent valuations arising outside this context, as with most brand valuations. I would argue that the greater need is for more *relevant* information, hence the profession should embrace the use of independent valuations at the initial recognition stage of an asset. I acknowledge that valuations are inherently subjective but I also acknowledge that their omission from the balance sheet is making a 'nonsense' of it. So, for example, in our annual Brand Finance reports, in which Tony has had some involvement, we have regularly pointed to the widening gap between accounting book values and market values in support of this argument.

Tony's book is different. It contains very little about brand valuation. It focuses on the asset recognition criteria used by accountants for disclosure purposes. It is based on some very simple but nevertheless compelling propositions; for example, that asset *recognition* should not be on the basis of a *measurement*, as it is at present, because recognition is logically prior to measurement. Thus, asset recognition should not be constrained by the accounting requirement for transaction-based measurements, allowing many more intangible assets to be recognised and capitalised as such. The issue of measurement then becomes subsequent to the process of asset recognition and, of course, the opportunity arises for the greater use of valuations. Obviously, that is good news from our viewpoint. In fact, this is where we return to the *relevance* argument, in that the real challenge facing the accounting profession is how to regulate for valuations. This book weakens the existing foundations on which accounting stands and simultaneously strengthens our position as brand valuers. You need to put on your thinking cap for this book—it's a powerful read.

David Haigh
Chief executive, Brand Finance plc

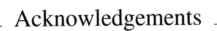

Acknowledgements

This book is largely a consolidation of several journal articles written by me, as cited in the references. I wish to express my thanks to the publishers of those articles for permission to use them in this book. I also wish to thank the business development director of Pannell Kerr Forster for permission to publish a small survey and to the accountants who completed it. The views expressed here do not necessarily reflect the corporate views of PKF. Finally, I wish to thank David Haigh, chief executive of Brand Finance plc, for his financial sponsorship of some of my research.

1
Introduction

The decision by the overwhelming majority of UK companies not to recognise and disclose brands as assets, brand assets, on their balance sheets is an issue in which managements, as financial information users, have a stake. Firstly, brands that are not recognisable as assets can end up being recognised as expenses instead, and as every manager knows, expenses should be cut as much as possible. Secondly, managers should not be left ignorant of the financial impact that these and other intangible assets can have on a business. For example, a very common measure of business performance is the return on investment (ROI), the investment often being restricted to balance sheet assets and therefore incomplete with regard to the return on many undisclosed intangible assets.

There is nothing new about the existence of a financial information gap in respect of intangibles and brands; that is, between the needs and concerns of financial information users, such as management and marketers, and the provision of that information by the accounting profession. For example, the Chartered Institute of Marketing (1993) expressed the following frustration:

> It is not the acceptance of brand equity which has been at the heart of the debate; it is whether accounting practices can adapt to a changing business environment in which 'worth' is typified by a set of intangible assets. This is an issue which our accounting colleagues show a persistent lack of commitment to resolve. And resolved it should be.

There are those interest groups outside the accounting profession, such as brand valuation companies, who point to the information gap between accounting book values and market values as evidence of missing intangible assets from the balance sheet (e.g. Brand Finance 2000). It has to be said, however, in defence of the accounting profession, that the accounts created by them have never purported to fill this gap through the exclusive use of market values. They have always comprised mixed measurement bases—see the Statement of Principles, paragraph B6.5 (ASB 1999). Also, as Gu and Lev (2001) point out, it assumes that there is no mispricing in capital markets. Investors who acquired internet shares in 1999, to see them fall in 2000, would obviously have a different view. Nevertheless, the gap cannot be due to measurement-related issues alone. The rise in the importance of branding and similar intellectual and/or artistic pursuits in the wealth-creating process and the lack of any notable rise in the disclosure of related intangible assets, other than recently in respect of purchased goodwill, appear to attest to restrictive accounting policies and practices. This assertion is supported by reference to a longitudinal survey of accounting practices in Chapter 5.

There is a strong financial information user perspective that seeks to justify why intangible assets should be disclosed in financial statements. Regardless of whether accountants choose to disclose intangible assets or not, the literature on intellectual capital indicates that considerable attention is now being directed towards the management of the wealth-creating potential of intangible assets, and the measurement of that wealth outside the existing accounting asset recognition boundary. Worryingly for accountants, there are also many metrics used in connection with intangibles which are not necessarily financially oriented and which therefore do not need to be controlled by accountants at all (e.g. Davidson 1999).

However, as a counter-argument, it can be said that most non-financial metrics, such as those presented in Kaplan and Norton's (1992) balanced scorecard, can ultimately be expressed in terms of financial metrics. For example, measures of customer satisfaction with a brand and measures of perceived quality can manifest themselves in terms of increased sales revenue and cost savings, respectively. In other words, it can be argued that financial metrics reign supreme and that this dominance could, to some extent, be used to capture control of the non-financial metrics currently created and used by those outside the purview of many in the accounting profession. Unfortunately, it would also appear that there are many in the accounting profession who do not see the need to seize this opportunity, preferring instead to retain the security blanket of their own regulatory environment. Of course, problems arise when others begin to perceive that the regulatory environment is increasingly unreflective of business reality, a reality indisputably inclusive of many intangible assets.

One of the attractions of money, other than spending it, is that it is a widely used proxy measure for most business activities. It enables accountants to compare the disparate worth of expenditure on a machine, in relation to expenditure on an advertising campaign, in a manner that is not possible with non-financial metrics. In contrast, many non-financial measures are company-specific and are not convertible within the same company, let alone between companies. So, for example, it is reasonable to assume that a positive measure of innovation may have a positive effect on a measure of customer performance and may have a positive effect on financial performance in whatever way a company chooses to measure it. But establishing cause and effect is a bit like adding apples to pears to equal oranges—the metrics do not mix. Perhaps, in this regard alone, we should call such attempts the unbalanced scorecard?

Despite the convertibility of money, as a single metric it can never capture the totality of business reality. Consider the machine/advertising example and whether comparisons of financial worth capture the reality of each activity. Clearly not. Yet users are, to a large extent, content to receive a picture of business reality in terms of money for reporting purposes. For now, financial metrics still dominate, and the accounting profession needs to use the power it has over them to paint a new picture of business reality which is inclusive of a wide variety of intangible assets. And yes, it can be done. Purchased goodwill is now capitalised as an asset, as per FRS10 (ASB 1997) on goodwill and intangible assets. Pre 1998 it was written off to reserves. Yet there was very little conceptual justification advanced as to its newly found status as an asset, post 1997. If accountants can sidestep the fundamental issue of whether purchased goodwill is an asset or not, and simply regulate it into existence (acquisition method) and out of existence (merger method) then they are not kings, but gods, in the realm of financial regulation. They change the perceived financial reality at their whim until the day when some rebellious mortal challenges their view of it. That day has now arrived and the worshippers are finding new craven images to worship in terms of balanced scorecards, data warehousing systems and the like.

This book is different from others in that instead of adopting a common user usefulness perspective that justifies the disclosure of intangible assets, it adopts the opposite perspective in asking why intangible assets are not being disclosed by the accounting profession.

Some may regard it as an attack on the methods of the accounting profession. If so, it is long overdue. The more enlightened will realise that unless the accounting profession responds to the needs for more information in respect of intangibles, it risks being sidelined by the rest of the business community, who are clearly intent on creating and managing alternative sources of non-financial information. Of necessity it must delve into accounting asset recognition issues in some depth. In this regard, it is worth distinguishing between the 'accounting' recognition and measurement of intangible assets leading to their capitalisation and disclosure on the balance sheet, and the 'general' recognition and measurement of intangibles, which occurs largely outside the accounting profession.

The 'brand asset' title of the book is deliberate since it examines the nature of an asset and whether a brand can qualify as one according to some criteria. If, as one of the most problematic of intangibles, it qualifies as an asset then it is likely to be capable of extension to many other intangibles and the 'door is opened' for their disclosure on the balance sheet. The book is therefore split into two parts in respect of 'assets' and 'brands' as assets. Part One addresses the following asset-related issues:

- The existing regulatory framework within which the accounting disclosure of intangible assets currently takes place and the cognitive assumptions underpinning such disclosure.
- The problems with the existing asset recognition criteria, particularly in respect of the requirement for recognisable 'past transactions or events' and also the important issue of separability.
- The dilemma of cost-based or valuation-based approaches to the measurement of intangible assets.
- The restrictive impact of FRS10 on the accounting disclosure of intangible assets.

In Part One I am trying to undermine the support given in everyday accounting practice by a root definition of accountancy: the UK accounting definition of an asset, which is also similar to the US definition. That definition is as follows: 'Assets are rights or other access to future economic benefits controlled by an entity as a result of past transactions or events' (ASB 1999, p. 50). It is tantamount to pulling the bottom brick out the wall; it produces some serious cracking in the edifice of accounting. It is perhaps not the wisest thing to do if one wishes to win friends within the accounting profession. Nevertheless, I attempt to show that in order for the accounting profession to embrace the widespread recognition of intangibles, it is going to have to reappraise the existing criteria for the recognition and measurement of an asset, starting with this root definition. Indeed, how can consensus ever be achieved between the users and preparers of financial information if they have different views on something as fundamental as what constitutes an asset? One can write about the management of intangibles as wealth-creating assets, and many do, but if one is not too sure whether something is an intangible asset or not, it becomes questionable whether such efforts are being focused in the right direction.

In Part Two I address two important requirements for the capitalisation of brands. Firstly, insofar as brand assets already appear on the balance sheet, they do so as an extraction from purchased goodwill. I cannot think of another situation where the disclosure of one type of asset, brand assets, is so heavily dependent on the existence of another 'asset', purchased goodwill, unless it is not actually dependent on its asset status, rather on its transaction-based existence. Now, that is a pragmatic consideration addressed in Chapter 4. I attempt to show in Part Two that, conceptually, purchased goodwill is not an asset and therefore any extraction of another asset from it is nonsensical. Secondly,

I advance the idea of recognising intangible assets on the basis of an artefact within an expanded asset recognition boundary created by the requirement for a legally separable identity. I provide a new definition of a brand asset that meets these requirements.

In Part Three I address, selectively, the politics surrounding the introduction of FRS10 based on the responses to the Accounting Standards Board's public hearings into goodwill and intangible assets. It provides some truly revealing insights into the process of standard setting in respect of intangibles. From my point of view it is dynamite! For example, one member commented on the lack of theoretically based reasoning in the submissions to the board. It is an omission I attempt to redress in this book.

The analysis for the above chapters is based on empirical evidence from a longitudinal survey of company accounts over the past eight years; selected results from a small questionnaire survey of chartered accountants; a number of descriptive frameworks adapted from the literature on jurisprudence, politics and accounting; and a literature review which includes the responses to the ASB's public hearings on the topic.

According to the Accounting Standards Board's working paper on goodwill and intangible assets (ASB 1995a, p. 9), 'intangible assets should be *identified* where control over the future economic benefits that they represent is apparent either through legal protection, such as a trademark or patent, or through physical custody, such as keeping secret intellectual property, e.g. a formula. *Identified* intangible assets should be *recognised* where management believes that it can make a reliable estimate of the asset's fair value' (original emphasis). Identification, de facto, means that one has recognised something unless recognition, above, is applied selectively for accounting purposes from what has been identified. In the case of intangibles this is on the basis of a 'reliable estimate of the asset's fair value', a measurement. However, measurement is logically subsequent to recognition otherwise one cannot be too sure what one is measuring. Nevertheless, reliability of measurement is the basis of recognition for intangibles and support for this stance is underpinned by the 'dog analogy' and the accounting notion of 'measurement separability' (Napier and Power 1992).

The dog analogy says that if something smells like a dog and it growls like a dog then it must be a dog. One does not need to see it or touch it to know that it is a dog. However, it could be wolf or, worse still, it could be a recording of a dog and therefore it is preferable that one sees it to recognise it. The medical profession would not adopt the same stance: it smells like urine but it turns out to be gangrene! Of course, the parallel argument in respect of intangibles is that one cannot see that which, by nature, is invisible unless one develops a mechanism for making it visible, in respect of this book, by means of a surrogate artefact. Measurement separability, on the other hand, asserts that if we can measure the intangible then the question of whether or not we can identify it as an asset is pre-empted. We have identified it by virtue of measuring. In effect, the three stages of identification, recognition and measurement are collapsed together. However, Archer (1994) comments, 'The issue of recognition per se is best regarded as logically prior to the issue of "measurability".'

A MORE ORDERED APPROACH

Step 1: Definition not identification

We should not *identify*, above, *what is* an intangible asset, we should *define* what *should be* an intangible asset because 'what is' does not exist unless society first decrees that it 'should be' and defines boundaries for its existence. All intangible assets are socially dependent assets. The logic is as follows: the human capital identified in the creation of tangible assets is converted into structural capital and physically remains as such after that society ceases to exist. In contrast, the human capital employed in the creation of intangible assets can also be converted into structural assets (patents, trademarks, etc.), but such assets continue to rely on human institutions for their perpetuation as assets and cannot exist independently of society. It follows, if those institutions cease to exist or if they refuse to identify intangible assets then there are no intangible assets. Thus, for example, the identification of a brand is initially dependent on marketers and legislators to determine what *should be* a brand and its related trademark, respectively, and then on lawyers to protect *what is* identified as a legally defensible asset. And finally, to a lesser extent, on accountants to account for its worth. Each institution expresses its own ideas on the identification of what *should be*, which in the case of the accounting disclosure of brands is applied very selectively and thereby restrictively.

Setting boundaries or limits to what 'should be' is really what 'identification' is all about. Subsequently, recognition of 'what is' occurs within these boundaries. For accountants this is usually done by definitions and standards. It has to be so because there are many items outside the accounting domain that can qualify as an asset and one needs to be clear about what is inside/outside this domain. As accountants communicate financial reality, so they effectively communicate that reality for the users of it; Ruth Hines (1988, 1991) has written two excellent papers on these issues.

Step 2: Asset recognition before asset measurement

In effect, this is asset recognition according to a defined nature. Where an intangible asset is purchased, asset recognition is within the existing transaction- or event-based boundary, as per the UK definition of an asset. Where an intangible asset is internally generated or where an asset is created by government edict, or where an asset is a 'windfall' gain, it tends not to be recognised within the existing transactions or events boundary. If, as a consequence, accountants decide to expand the existing asset recognition boundary, the issue remains as to what should trigger recognition of an intangible asset. For example, should a boundary be inclusive of internally created intellectual property in the traditional sense of items like patents, trademarks and copyrights, and exclusive of other 'softer' intangibles such as reputation, strategic locations and superior management? Actually, intellectual property can be interpreted very widely by the courts to include many items that accountants would traditionally regard as expenses, not assets. So, when the ASB refers to identification through 'legal protection', it needs to be careful about what is actually being identified.

The book proposes asset recognition on the basis of an artefact. In effect, making the intangible tangible through the creation of a man-made surrogate. The artefact is recognised within a boundary established by the requirement for an accounting asset to have a legally separable identity. Most transactions (the existing asset recognition boundary) possess this characteristic, so it is simply a development of what already exists.

Step 3: Measurement of the intangible asset

The measurement of the worth of intangible assets can be 'accurately wrong' through adherence to transaction-based cost measurements, which are accurately verifiable but, over time, lose their relevance. Alternatively, one can be 'approximately right' through the use of current valuations with all the attendant subjectivity of a valuations approach to accounting. One can also undertake both at the same time through acceptance of mixed measurement bases. So, for example, one can give prominence to the balance sheet through the argument that accounts should show the increase or decrease in the worth of assets over a period of account but allow mixed measurement bases to be used as the means of portraying changes in that worth. Mixed measurement means there is little hope for comparability between accounts. The tension between a transaction-based view and a valuation-based view has been at the heart of considerable debate within accounting, e.g. SSAP16 on current cost accounting (ASC 1980). This book does not provide a solution to this thorny issue. If it did, I would not be an impoverished academic. Its contribution is primarily directed towards definition and recognition on the basis that it is logically prior to do so, even in respect of intangibles where recognition is somewhat problematic.

The existing asset recognition and measurement criteria are founded to a large extent on legal criteria (ASB 1999) and it is therefore reasonable to examine these criteria to see whether they can embrace the totality of what lawyers call intellectual property and what accountants call intangible assets. This matters to lawyers if only so they may have some idea of the value of these problematic assets for litigation purposes. It also matters to accountants because of the influence that case law and statute can have on developments in intangible asset accounting.

If one is to consider asset recognition boundaries and what may be captured and measured within them, an obvious first question is, What are the boundaries? Secondly, how do these boundaries differ, if at all, between the accounting profession and the legal profession, for example, in their respective comprehension of the terms 'intangible assets' and 'intellectual property' and in their representation, in part or whole, of the intellectual capital employed in a business? This is addressed in the next chapter. It is important because I have proposed a revised asset recognition boundary based on the notion of legal separability and therefore the legal and accounting viewpoints on intangibles should be compared. The terms 'intangible assets' and 'intellectual property' are often used interchangeably, yet an examination of some definitions in this regard would indicate that they should not be used in this way.

Part One
Assets

2

An alternative approach to the accounting definition of an asset

According to Gerboth (1987), the existence of definitions matters 'hardly at all in deciding most issues of real-world consequence. Their contribution is to add brevity to discourse.' Other disciplines are not even concerned about the precision of their definitions. Popper (1962), in respect of science, argues that 'the view that the precision of science and of its scientific language depends on the precision of its terms is certainly very plausible, but it is none the less I believe, a mere prejudice. The precision of a language depends rather, just on the fact that it takes care not to burden its terms with task of being precise.' We have all experienced the situation where, for example, one believes that they have communicated clearly and precisely information to another, only to find their understanding and interpretation of it is different to what was communicated. That said, there is still a role for definitions in a narrow sense, such as in determining whether a patient is in a persistent vegetative state or not.

The comparison to be drawn, however, is with the legal profession. Legal definitions are a useful basis for instruction, but any attempt to reduce judgements to a number of deductions from definitions or other principles could easily lead to the occasional miscarriage of justice. It is for that reason parties are able to seek equitable remedies where a strict application of 'principle' would lead to injustice. The desire for the logic and structure offered by definitions and principles is deeply rooted in the human psyche, for as Holmes (1897) states:

> The logical method and form flatter that longing for certainty and for repose which is in every human mind. But certainty generally is illusion, and repose is not the destiny of man. Behind the logical form lies a judgement as to the relative worth and importance of competing legislative grounds, often an inarticulate and unconscious judgement, it is true, and yet the very root and nerve of the whole proceeding.

In essence, it is the personal responsibility of the individual, whether lawyer, accountant or other professional man/woman, who, in making a decision, searches for the best possible approximation of truth at that moment.

I seek, notwithstanding the comments of Gerboth and Popper above, to use a definition of intellectual capital, intellectual property and intangible assets as the starting point for an examination of their respective recognition boundaries. I do this because the terms are often used interchangeably and, as will be shown later on, they are not the same things and thus there is a need for a greater clarity of understanding of these terms.

INTELLECTUAL CAPITAL

According to Dzinkowski (2000), intellectual capital is a broad-based term that has many complex connotations and is often used synonymously with intellectual property, intellectual assets and knowledge assets: 'Intellectual capital can be thought of as the ...

knowledge-based equity that the company possesses. As such, intellectual capital can be both the end result of a knowledge transformation process or the knowledge itself that is transformed into intellectual property or intellectual assets of the firm.' The growth of internet companies and brand valuation companies is, for example, testimony to the opportunities that have arisen from this knowledge transformation process. This is what Quah (1997) refers to as a 'weightless' economic sector: 'In a weightless economy, success comes not from having built the largest factory, the biggest oil super-tanker, or the longest production line. In a weightless economy, success comes from knowing how to organise understanding into forms that others will demand.' The sentiment is clear—the real wealth creators are increasingly intangible in nature.

Intellectual capital can be analysed into what may be argued are its constituent parts: human, customer/relational and organisational/structural (Edvinson and Malone 1997). It is through the interplay of these three types of intellectual capital that value is supposedly created. Examples are given in Table 2.1, which is by no means comprehensive.

Within the knowledge-based literature a distinction is made between explicit and tacit knowledge. Artefacts, such as an encoded diskette or document, are the means by which information is made physical, identifiable and transferable, that is, explicit. Explicit knowledge can be purchased, repeated, reinvented and stolen—it resides separately from the individual or group. On the other hand, tacit knowledge refers to the real-time, often subconscious, cognitive and other reasoning processes that we utilise and take for granted in the completion of our day-to-day lives. We rely on similar past experiences, fill in the gaps by using these processes and then we make a decision on the best forward strategy. Unless shared with a community, tacit knowledge dies with the individual. However, the act of sharing tacit knowledge always creates something new. Tacit knowledge drives the creativity that is so vital for innovative companies.

Table 2.1 Types of intellectual capital

Human Capital	Customer (Relational) Capital
1. Know-how	1. Brands
2. Education	2. Customers
3. Vocational qualifications	3. Company names
4. Work-related knowledge	4. Backlog orders
5. Occupational assessments	5. Distribution channels
6. Psychometric assessments	6. Business collaborations
7. Work-related competencies	7. Licensing agreements
8. Entrepreneurial elan, innovativeness, proactive and reactive abilities, changeability	8. Favourable contracts
	9. Franchising agreements

Organisational (Structural) Capital

Intellectual property	*Infrastructure assets*
1. Patents	1. Management philosophy
2. Copyrights	2. Corporate culture
3. Design rights	3. Management processes
4. Trade secrets	4. Information systems
5. Trademarks	5. Networking systems
6. Service marks	6. Financial relations

Source: Dzinkowski (2000)

The accounting profession has already explored the idea of people as assets under the heading of human resource accounting (Brummet *et al.* 1968, 1969a 1969b); that is, recognition of their tacit knowledge and the skills resident in individuals themselves. Most of the accounting focus has been directed towards measurement methods as a means of asset recognition and establishing a value. Many of these measures also include composite non-monetary value measures such as job satisfaction indices and labour turnover rates (e.g. Likert and Pyle 1971). However, Scarpello and Theeke (1989, p. 267) state:

> Human resource value is a construct for which there are, at best, weak empirical measures. Good science requires that any surrogate measures proposed for a construct be tested to demonstrate both that they are proper substitutes and that they can be reliably measured. Unless, the construct, human resource value, is associated with empirical referents (that is, real world measures), and unless these measures are tested, all attempts to model human resource accounting (HRA) conceptual frameworks simply deteriorate into mathematical exercises.

Other relevant sources are Gambling (1974), Friedman and Lev (1974) and Jaggi and Lau (1974). As a consequence, they recommend:

> Until advocates of HRA can demonstrate valid generalisable means for measuring human resource value in monetary terms, researchers abandon further consideration of the possible benefits from HRA. (Scarpello and Theeke 1989, p. 275)

A call for more empirical research with better experimental controls was supported by Sackmann *et al.* (1989). However, Turner's (1996) comment that HRA 'has progressed at something less than a snail's pace in the past two decades' is probably still accurate.

According to Ulf Johanson (1999), there is a need for better transparency of investments in human capital. In citing an OECD (1996) report, he states the implication is that human capital measurement and accounting for human resources have to be further improved. However, the argument developed here is that the definition and recognition criteria for intangibles need to be established first as a conceptual basis, before any consideration is given to the process of measurement. Therein lies the problem; intellectual capital may indeed be the knowledge-based equity that a company possesses but defining, recognising and measuring separable aspects of knowledge in its tacit form is virtually impossible. It has therefore to be acknowledged that the wealth-creating potential of human capital in its tacit form is very unlikely to be recognised by the accounting profession, because of the absence of verifiable evidence as to its existence and also the aforementioned difficulties in measuring it.

INTELLECTUAL PROPERTY

Intellectual property is property, something that can be owned and dealt with. It refers to the legal rights associated with creativity or business reputation and goodwill (Bainbridge 1994). Legal rights are interpreted widely here to include items such as reputation for which there is no legally determined artefact to represent its existence. This distinction, however, is not clear from Table 2.1 since all the items listed under 'intellectual property' require an artefact, for example, a documented patent registration. So an obvious question to consider is whether the existence of an artefact simultaneously means the item is both explicit knowledge and is also an item of intellectual property. If so, it would exclude commercial reputation and perhaps goodwill as items of intellectual property—there are no artefacts for them.

A competitor who, for example, seeks deliberately to undermine an internally established distribution channel or management process by computer hacking (both specified in Table 2.1), and thereby damages the reputation or goodwill of the business, is infringing legal rights. That is, even though no artefact is readily identifiable in respect of the distribution channel, management process, reputation or goodwill. Similarly, remedies may be available in respect of the damage done to reputation and goodwill through the tort of passing off. So it would initially appear that intellectual property rights do not have to be supported by an artefact. However, unlike the 'intellectual property' items listed in Table 2.1, the artefacts in this example are created by a legal judgement. In other words, it takes some form of legal action to establish the proven legal right that turns what was tacit knowledge, and would normally remain as such, into explicit knowledge documented as a court order. Also any damages in this example are assessed in relation to reputation and goodwill; the knowledgeable use of the internally created distribution channel or management process remains as tacit knowledge unless subsequently patented. Further, whether such court-ordered rights in respect of reputation and goodwill are separable, in the sense that they can be transferred to a third party, is very unlikely. What this example highlights here is the importance of artefacts in the legal recognition of intellectual property and what they do in terms of setting an artefact-based intellectual property recognition boundary.

Where knowledge is made explicit then the attachment of legal rights is usually an issue of formality, such as trademarking a brand. Where the knowledge is tacit then the attachment of legal rights is, as demonstrated in the previous paragraph, far more problematic. Generally speaking, there are no legal rights that can be attached to the tacit knowledge in a person's mind, and therefore no intellectual property exists. However, it does raise an interesting question as to whether human capital itself can sometimes be regarded as intellectual property. For example, one could attempt to argue that the specific contractual arrangements related to restraint of trade agreements and advanced musical recording contracts try to convert, in advance, the tacit knowledge still resident in a person's mind into the explicit knowledge of respectively not doing or doing some future thing. The artefacts in both cases are documentary.

It is bit like taking an intellectual property option on a person where the intent is, respectively, to protect and promote access to future economic benefits. The difficulty of placing a value on doing (or not doing) some future thing, particularly in respect of musical composition, is axiomatic but, nevertheless, is undertaken frequently in the music industry. However, in general, human capital cannot be formalised in the same way that a patent can be, unless one believes in forced slavery. Even then, property ownership of the person is not the same thing as the ownership of the intellectual property resident in that person's mind.

To summarise so far, the money invested in employing intellectual capital within a business may be recognised as intellectual property where an artefact is attached to it. This may be attached by statutory registration such as trademarking, legal documentation such as patents, court order or by some other legal means that provides the intellectual property so recognised with a legally defensible, physically represented identity. Insofar as the intellectual capital invested in a business exists but is not recognisable other than in an explicit knowledge form, it is not regarded as intellectual property. Clearly, this represents a narrow view of what would comprise the intellectual capital employed in a business from a legal viewpoint. However, it is also incomplete. Let us look more closely at the interface between the accounting profession and the legal profession by reference to transactions.

The above summary excludes the artefact of documentation that typically accompanies most transactions—a purchase order, invoice, receipt, cheque stub, etc., whatever asset or expense represented thereby is made explicit. Clearly, a tangible asset or an expense such as an electricity bill is not intellectual property. It is at the juncture of asset and expense that the problems arise; that is, where the absence of tangibility suggests that something should be expensed immediately but which is, nevertheless, contributing to future economic benefits over many years like its tangible asset counterparts. For example, an architect's drawing of a building is an expense if the related building is not built. However, it is an integral part of the building asset cost if it is actually built.

Yet the distinction is irrelevant from an intellectual property viewpoint. The order/invoice for the drawing is an artefact that is sufficient for recognition of the property to take place; so too, for example, where a brand is purchased. Obviously, in both cases, their status as items of intellectual property is 'improved' where they are copyrighted and trademark documented, respectively, in addition to their order/invoices. They will also be better protected from copying by competitors. The conclusion to be drawn is that intellectual property can embrace what accountants may regard as an expense. So, for example, one can purchase the right to own or access the aforementioned distribution channel or management process, and these thereby become items of intellectual property to lawyers and, in all probability, expenses to the accountant. This would suggest that the recognition boundary of what may be regarded as intellectual property is broader than in respect of intangible assets.

INTANGIBLE ASSETS

The UK accounting definition of intangible assets is that they are 'non-financial fixed assets that do not have physical substance but are identifiable and are controlled by the entity through custody or legal rights' (ASB 1997). Why intangible assets are 'non-financial' is not clear. An interpretation is that they have no financial value but this must be incorrect or they would not be assets at all. One troubling feature of this definition is that there is no apparent linkage to the standard UK accounting definition of an asset as 'rights or other access to *future economic benefits controlled* by an entity as a result of *past transactions or events*' (ASB 1999, p. 50; original emphasis); that is, unless one regards the reference to 'non-financial fixed assets' as a subset of the asset definition in total. However, it is still unclear whether the term 'non-financial' is reconcilable with the asset requirement to produce 'future economic benefits' as intimated earlier. Further, if it is a subset, then there is also an apparent conflict between the two defined means of control unless, perhaps, 'custody or legal rights' is a subset of the term 'events'. However, in interpreting events as legal rights one would end up with a circular asset definition with 'rights' at the beginning and the end of it.

One final criticism of this linkage, if any, between the above definitions is that the intangible asset definition is a constitutive definition. It attempts to define what it is by nature. In contrast, the UK asset definition is not constitutive, nor operational as a definition. Apologies for the vagueness of this statement, which requires an explanation.

It attempts to define what an asset is by nature (constitutive) but that nature is actually expressed in terms of what an asset does (operational); that is, it produces future economic benefits. According to this definition, for example, advertising expenditure, that is, revenue expenditure not capital expenditure, is an asset because it can produce future economic benefits and is the result of past transactions or events. Of the two definitional types, one suspects that the UK asset definition is more in the nature of an operational definition, and therefore it is difficult to reconcile with the constitutive definition of an intangible asset. In exploring further, the construction of the UK asset definition is assumed to be the dominant definition in the accounting disclosure of intangible assets on published financial statements.

There are three key features of the UK asset definition which are underlined above. Incidentally, these are the same key features of the US asset definition (FASB 1985). As shown earlier, the term 'future economic benefits' is a very broad term. Also it does not prejudice any particular measurement basis—cost or valuation. It is also a nebulous term because 'economic' and 'benefits' are words that are capable of multiple interpretations, separately and jointly. In some ways it is actually a good idea to have a broad term because it offers flexibility to the user of it and avoids the sort of introspective distinctions that are the lifeblood of lawyers.

This broad term, however, is bounded by a narrower and largely legal requirement for asset recognition to be the result of past transactions or events. The term 'transactions' is easy to comprehend, manifests itself typically in terms of purchases/sales and is, overwhelmingly, the principal means of establishing the existing accounting asset recognition boundary. The term 'events' used to be interpreted narrowly in terms of legal obligations such as a judgement debtor or an insurance claim, but now it is interpreted more widely to include discovery, growth, extraction, processing or innovation (ASB 1999, p. 64). Together, the terms have created a very robust recognition boundary that has served the accounting profession well for many decades. It has also recently been expanded to include the limited disclosure of intangible assets on the basis of recognition of a readily ascertainable market value, or RAMV (ASB 1997).

However, it has still not kept pace with a changing society in which intellectual capital employed, as well as financial capital employed, is now an important resource in the creation of wealth. That is because unless it is made explicit, the intellectual creativity underpinning intellectual capital remains with the individual and therefore is unlikely to be represented by intangible assets captured within a transaction- or event-based asset recognition boundary. Generally, if one is going to transact for an intangible asset, the knowledge presented thereby needs to be explicitly represented by an artefact, otherwise it remains in its tacit form and therefore difficult to identify for transaction purposes.

Yet, as in the earlier advertising 'asset' example, the accounting profession has an advantage in this regard because for audit purposes every transaction is usually documented in some way. It thereby presents a legally supportable artefact for any would-be intangible asset, even if that 'asset' is normally regarded as an expense. Indeed, at its discretion, the accounting profession can capitalise and disclose virtually any tacit knowledge as an intangible asset by reference to a directly, and sometimes indirectly, related transaction. Thus, in this latter regard, a software programmer's time and related revenue expense may be capitalised as an asset in substitution for the software intangible asset itself. The artefact of an electronically encoded diskette, patent letters and/or copyright is not regarded as an asset in the same way as lawyers would regard this as intellectual property, nor is its worth subject to valuation. Instead, the programmer's labour cost is capitalised as a substitute because it is the only element that is transaction-based. Even then, in many cases the expense is not recognised at all as an asset but as revenue expenditure to the profit and loss account. For example, Bill Gates, Microsoft's chief executive, was quoted as saying, 'Our primary assets, which are our software and our software-development skills, do not show up on the balance sheet at all' (*Economist*, 12 June 1994, p. 94).

SUMMARY

To summarise, the broadly based economic notion of an asset being rights or access to future economic benefits is bounded or limited by a predominantly legally based requirement for those benefits to be recognised within accounting by means of transactions or events. It was argued that within this boundary the accounting profession is able to capitalise and disclose many of the examples presented in Table 2.1, and more, if it chooses to do so. Instead, there were many anomalies where expenses were capitalised and many assets that were not capitalised, and vice versa. Part of the reason for this situation is the operating nature of an asset definition that does not allow one to distinguish according to a defined nature between capital and revenue expenditure or, specifically, between revenue expenditure and intangible assets. Perhaps the comment of Egginton (1990) is particularly pertinent in this regard: 'The biggest hurdle for recognition of intangibles may be an innate preference for tangible assets in accounting conventions, rather than questions of expected future economic benefits or whether magnitudes are sufficiently reliable for recognition.'

I have attempted to highlight the importance of recognition of either an intangible asset or intellectual property being determined on the basis of a legally defensible artefact. The artefact is the means of giving explicit physical form to tacit knowledge, which by its nature is intangible. The strength of 'legal defensibility' is initially determined by the method or form used to create the artefact. The strongest forms are perhaps where the knowledge is presented in pictorial form, such as a documented trademark, and/or with a precise description, such as a patent. The weakest form is perhaps where the knowledge is purchased as a transaction, for example, the right to use a computer-based information network, and the artefacts take the form of commercial documentation such as a purchase order and invoice. There can sometimes be more than one artefact, as when an established patent is purchased.

The existence of an artefact enables the legal profession to recognise the item as intellectual property regardless of whether the accounting profession regards the item so recognised as an expense or an asset. The interpretation of what is to be captured within an intellectual property recognition boundary therefore appears to be wider than in respect of the interpretation of what is to be caught within an intangible asset's recognition boundary. The legal remedies are widely based too. They can be direct as with a trademark infringement or indirect, as when the reputation or goodwill is damaged by damage to an item of intellectual property. In contrast, the accounting profession tends to recognise an intangible asset only where there is an identifiable transaction. Thus, many non-transaction-based intangibles remain unrecognised, examples being given earlier.

It is just as important to highlight what is wrong with the existing accounting definition of an asset as it is to advance the notion of asset recognition on the basis of an artefact within an expanded asset recognition boundary; that is, one bounded by the requirement for an asset to have a legally separable identity. Otherwise, there is little incentive to change. In Chapter 3 I would like to address some of the cognitive assumptions that underpin the way accountants view assets. Also I would like to show, in a somewhat cursory manner, by reference to a small questionnaire, that I am not alone in my concerns over the existing definition of an asset.

3

Cognitive assumptions behind the accounting recognition of assets

Selected responses to a questionnaire on the definition of an asset have been 'interwoven' with selected and developed elements of a politics-based work on ideology by Hamilton (1987). This provides some empirical support for an examination of the cognitive assumptions underpinning the accounting recognition of assets. It is an examination which shows that the definition of an asset is not a static thing and that it should reflect changing business circumstance, particularly in respect of the recognition of intangible assets. After providing some background information on the questionnaire survey, the remaining two sections of this chapter investigate the aforementioned cognitive assumptions and provide examples of the changing nature of an asset within the context of changing economic situations within society. The aim is to 'soften up the ground' by showing that assets are not static things, prior to an examination of what I regard as the most restrictive element within the existing asset definitions—to be addressed in the next chapter.

THE QUESTIONNAIRE SURVEY

A questionnaire on the definition of an asset was circulated, internally, among 294 chartered accountants at 18 offices of PKF, throughout the UK. It is emphasised that the views expressed here in no way reflect the corporate views of PKF, merely the selective views of a small number of their accountants. The perceived advantage of presenting the questionnaire internally was that the response rate would be improved. This proved to be correct. One hundred and seventeen responses were received, a 40% response rate. The disadvantage of an internally circulated questionnaire was the possibility of company policy bias. However, firstly and tentatively, it could be argued that a questionnaire on something as theoretical and basic (even dull) as the definition of an asset would be unlikely to be addressed strategically and, therefore, unlikely to be affected by company-specific policy issues. Secondly, the results were not invalid. They simply could not be generalised to the accounting population. Whilst regrettable, this was a worthwhile 'trade-off' for improving the response rate on a questionnaire which I knew required a high degree of personal perseverance. As a result, the statistical analysis was simplistic, percentages and the net sum of positive (agrees) over negative responses (disagrees). There was also a midpoint 'don't know' which was excluded from the analysis. This accounts for answers that can show, for example, a small favourable percentage but a positive balance.

Let us now consider the cognitive assumptions underlying the existing definitions of an asset and the problems associated with them. These are identified on a point-by-point basis as follows.

*The existing definitions of an asset represent a selective economics-based picture of
reality—only assets that produce future economic benefits are recognised by accountants*

The definition of an asset should, ideally, be set within a broad conceptual framework
so that the reasons for adopting a selective economic perspective can be understood,
for example, the US Statement of Financial Accounting Concepts Nos 1–6 (1978–85).
However, this simply broadens the debate to the point where the task becomes all-
absorbing, and defining the broader picture replaces the definition of relatively narrower
issues, such as the definition of an asset. If one accepts this argument then one must also
accept the possibility that the existing asset definitions may, as a consequence, represent
an incomplete view of the reality they seek to portray.

It is suggested that the selective economics-based picture of reality should not necessarily be conditioned by whether something produces future economic benefits. If an
asset exists, it exists by nature and not solely by what it produces—the future economic
benefits. This is a view that is partly supported by the following response:

	Agree (%)	Net +/−
It is possible for an asset to be capable of use for economic purposes and never actually be used for such purposes	72	+75

Seventy-two percent of respondents believed that it is possible to have the use of an asset
for economic purposes and never actually use it for such purposes. Consider a worked-out
opencast coal mine. A big hole is left in the ground with no apparent future economic
benefits to be obtained from it. Indeed, it could even be regarded as a liability in terms
of safety and reclamation. However, this is simply a question of perception since it is
possible to use the hole for something else, for example, a boating lake or landfill site.
The hole in the ground is still an asset irrespective of whether someone decides to use
it economically or not. Schuetze (1993) argues that to define an asset in terms of future
economic benefits is to refer to it in terms of a higher-order abstraction, which he asserts
is far removed from what the ordinary man understands to be an asset, for example, his
car or house. The definition is therefore focused on what an asset does, rather than on
what it is, according to its nature and/or resource. For example, a building can be defined
as providing shelter and security to those who use it; however, such a definition could
be equally applied to a helmet worn by a motorcyclist. On the other hand, recognition
according to an asset's nature and/or resource would enable it to be disclosed as such,
irrespective of its current ability to produce economic benefits.

The phrase 'future economic benefit' is an imprecise term ('economic' generally refers
to the creation of wealth and satisfaction of human wants). If, for example, the asset
definitions are actually referring to a future cash-flow-based picture of reality, then perhaps
this should be defined explicitly. In other words, the specific cash flow term should replace
the generic economic term since this is the actual way of portraying the existing versions of
economic reality. However, respondents did not share this view, with only 20% agreeing
that a method of measurement should be specified in the definition of an asset:

	Agree (%)	Net +/−
A method of measurement (e.g. cost or cash flow) should be specified in definition of an asset instead of the phrase 'future economic benefits'	20	−30

A related observation to the above charge of 'imprecision' is that 65% of respondents agree that the phrase 'future economic benefits' could be inclusive of bartering. Also 79% of respondents agree that the phrase 'future economic benefits' does not differentiate between capital and revenue expenditure:

	Agree (%)	Net +/−
'Future economic benefits' could be obtained through bartering for goods or services	65	+65
The phrase 'future economic benefits' does not differentiate between future economic benefits arising from capital expenditure or from revenue expenditure	79	+89
Expenditure on advertising can create 'future economic benefits'	81	+90

Failure to differentiate between an asset and an expense negates the usefulness of an asset definition, a point reinforced by the observation that 81% of respondents believed advertising expenditure can create future economic benefits, despite its current status as an expense rather than as an asset. Generally, respondents were unsure about the precision of the term 'future economic benefits':

	Agree (%)	Net +/−
The UK accounting definition of an asset refers to 'future economic benefits'. An 'economic benefit' can refer to a state benefit or charitable benefit	35	+5
The UK accounting definition of an asset refers to 'future economic benefits'. The meaning of the word 'economic' is unclear	34	+1

The existing definitions of an asset are created from an interconnected set of ideas

These interconnected ideas, for example, the linkage of 'future economic benefits' to 'transactions or events', gained acceptance through their consistent and logical association with each other. This will inevitably involve a subjective assessment of the consistency and logic of a definition, which will include objectives, structure and linguistic interpretations.

The definitional linkage of 'future economic benefits' to 'past transactions or events' provides two distinct views of balance sheet assets at the same time. One view is based on future cash flows (FCF), with or without a related transaction or event. The term 'future economic benefits' is broader than being a mere representation of cash flows; nevertheless, the principal expectation is that such benefits are used to generate future cash flows (ASB 1999, para 4.16). The other view is based on original/historic cost (HC). Whereas FCF can be established with or without reference to a transaction or event, HC can only be established by reference to a recognisable transaction or event. These views currently coexist as, for example, when the Hilton Group plc simultaneously capitalises new hotels at cost and existing hotels using discounted cash flows once the income streams become established. The initial recognition of an asset is based on HC and each hotel is separately recognisable. However, sometimes these two views of balance sheet assets do not easily coexist, as with goodwill (Baxter 1993).

Goodwill is inseparable from the other assets of a business. The HC is established as part of a transaction for the purchase of a business but changing the measurement to FCF for goodwill alone is a highly subjective exercise. It is also a highly problematic exercise because purchased goodwill mingles with internally generated goodwill such that the two become indistinguishable. Regardless of whichever measurement method best portrays economic reality, there is an inconsistency in accounting treatment which must raise doubts about the logic of the above linkage, if only from a comparability viewpoint.

In contrast, asset recognition based on recognition of an artefact within an expanded boundary bounded by the requirement for a legally separable identity, is also based on an interconnected set of ideas; that is, physical recognition of the artefact (surrogate artefacts in the case of intangibles) to their separable recognition within an expanded legally determined boundary (which would include most transactions or events). The advantage of this interconnected approach is that, firstly, it does not mix time frames—*future* economic benefits to *past* transactions. Secondly, it sets a physical/legal boundary within which to determine the nature of an asset. In Part Two I explore criteria for the recognition of this nature, of which the ability to produce income is but one of many fundamental characteristics. In other words, unlike a definition based on future economic benefits, it is not the only characteristic of an asset. Thirdly, it is not outcome driven. An asset does not have to produce future economic benefits to remain as an asset by nature—the big hole example, above. Thus within the requirements of the existing asset definition, purchased brands can be capitalised whereas internally created brands are seldom capitalised, because it would appear they do not initially arise from recognisable transactions or events. Yet the artefact-based approach recognises the related trademark as an asset irrespective of whether it is purchased or not. This inconsistency is also readily acknowledged by respondents, with 74% of them agreeing that internally created brands or software are assets irrespective of whether they arose from a transaction or an event:

	Agree (%)	Net +/−
A 'non-purchased' or internally created brand or software is an asset irrespective of whether its recognition was or was not the result of a 'transaction or event'	74	+74

Brand valuations often rely on discounted cash flow techniques. Provided such FCF-based valuations do not breach the amount of transaction-based HC of purchased goodwill, then a small number of companies will capitalise brands. A longitudinal survey of intangible asset accounting companies, including those who capitalise brands, is presented in Part Two. The FCF valuation is therefore constrained by HC, that is, the transaction-based cost of goodwill. The above economic benefit/transaction linkage of ideas is thereby not only reinforced, it also shows the dominance of a transaction-based HC over FCF approaches. Secondly, it emphasises the reluctance of the accounting profession to move away from a traditional double-entry, HC, transaction-based view of the balance sheet at the initial recognition stage of an asset.

An economics-based picture of reality means that certain groups in society may feel unable to accept it

An economic view of an asset, as a right or access to future economic benefits, will not necessarily coincide with a physicist's view of an asset, as a collection of atoms. Whilst it may be unnecessary to embrace every group in society, the ability of a definition to withstand criticism will be enhanced by its widespread acceptance. Conversely, unless one lives in an environment of sensory deprivation, it is impossible not to observe the assets that are all around us. How then can certain groups in society, such as the aforementioned physicists, feel unable to accept the existing accounting definition of an asset unless either the cognitive assumption is flawed or the definition, itself, is flawed? Only two definitions of an asset, as contained in Figure 3.1, seek to explain the nature of an asset, specifically in terms of 'resources'. This has not been universally adopted, probably because of the difficulties in defining an intangible asset's metaphysical properties. However, it could have been established in broad terms so that everyone in society was able to accept it. For example, an asset could have been defined as capital, land and labour (including intellectual property) or combinations thereof, that is, the economic factors of production. Even an 'ordinary' man would understand that his car or house comprised some of these attributes and it would also have perpetuated the overall economic perspective. That said, most respondents were ambivalent to the idea of including resources in a definition of an asset:

	Agree (%)	Net +/−
The resource(s) which constitute an asset, such as capital, land and labour, should be stated in the definition of an asset	29	−9

The existing definitions of an asset are functional

For an item to be regarded as an asset, the existing asset definitions require, among other things, the exercise of rights or access to or obtaining or control over future economic benefits. Consider the evidence in Figure 3.1.

No attempt is made to define an asset's constituent nature, other than as a resource. Assets are defined functionally as the action or purpose of a thing in a specified role. The role is defined as one that functionally provides rights or other access to future economic benefits, a broadly determined 'economic' role. It follows that if the role is broadly defined, so the actions and purposes may also be broadly determined. For example, the oil company which is creator and owner of an internally created patent for an inexpensive, clean, safe, unlimited supply of energy from sea water or cold fusion may simply do nothing with it

- An asset is a resource controlled by the enterprise as a result of past events and from which future economic benefits are expected to flow to the enterprise. (IASC 1989)
- Assets are resources or rights incontestably controlled by an entity at the accounting date that are expected to yield it future economic benefits. (Solomons 1989)
- Assets are probable future economic benefits obtained or controlled by a particular entity as a result of past transactions or events. (FASB 1985)
- Assets are rights or other access to future economic benefits controlled by an entity as a result of past transactions or events. (ASB 1999)

Figure 3.1   The accounting definitions of an asset

for the purposes of protecting its oil revenues. Potentially, the patent provides rights or access to substantial future economic benefits, nevertheless, it may be used to deny others the use of it or even to destroy it. As a consequence, other members of society pick up the cost for the continued use of oil in terms of pollution, medical consequences, and so on. Similarly, the fast-food company McDonald's enjoys rights or access to substantial future economic benefits from its internally created brand asset, which it aggressively protects against would-be copiers. The point here is that, despite complying with the above broadly defined economic role, these intangibles are not typically disclosed as assets on the balance sheet. Functionality, 'the rights or other access', is exercised selectively, one might say restrictively, within the broadly defined economic role with limited cognizance given to the alternatives, such as those raised in the questionnaire.

An alternative to a functional asset definition is one based on its constituent nature as discussed in terms of an artefact in the first section of this chapter. The implication of a constituent asset definition, rather than one based on economic outcomes, is that it could perhaps embrace the intellectual capital resource as well as the physical resources associated with the capital, land and labour.

Even within an 'economic' role, a number of specific roles can be identified which are not addressed by the definition of an asset:

	Agree (%)	Net $+/-$
It is an important feature of the UK accounting definition of an asset that it is capable of use for economic purposes	88	+97
It is possible to have the use of an asset for economic purposes which is intangible	90	+101
It is possible for an asset to be capable of use for economic purposes and never actually be used for such purposes	72	+75
It is possible to have the use of an asset for economic purposes without owning it	87	+98

	Agree (%)	Net +/−
It is possible to have the use of an asset for economic purposes which is a 'free good' (e.g. sea water) available for anyone to use	64	+56
Rights or access to an asset enables one to consume, destroy or waste it	62	+50
Rights or access to an asset enables one to impose costs on others, such as pollution costs	44	+20
Rights to an asset enables one to settle debts with it	41	+11
Rights to an asset enables one to deny others the use of it	62	+45

The response to these questions highlights the fact that the role of an asset is broader than that of just rights or access to future economic benefits. This is important because it is a contention expressed here that the accounting recognition of an asset based on a transaction or event is now too restrictive. Further, by showing the different ways of viewing an asset's role within a business, it may broaden the accounting profession's perception as to what constitutes an asset. I will show, for example, in the next section of this chapter, how some of these roles change as society changes. Certainly, in respect of intangible assets, the role now played by intangible assets in westernised societies has grown considerably with rapid technological developments and globalisation.

All of the above questionnaire responses were positive, which indicates unsurprisingly that accountants are aware of the wider role of assets within business than just for rights or access to future economic benefits, even if this has not yet translated into a revised definition of an asset.

The existing definitions of an asset contain statements of fact and/or statements of a normative nature

In attempting to portray economic reality, the existing definitions of an asset are bound to display some factual as well as normative characteristics associated with them. Often the two characteristics merge so that the factual characteristics underpin normative statements. For example, if increased cash flows are the factual observable effect of asset utilisation and control, then it could be argued, normatively, that there should also be a recognisable cause to that effect. Specifically, the definition of an asset should specify those characteristics of the nature of an asset that give rise to the effect, the increased cash flows. The selective combination of factual and normative statements to produce a definition represents a piecemeal approach to such a task. Whilst it can be used to great effect, one is never quite sure whether 'pieces of the jigsaw' are missing? In Part Two I make reference to a descriptive framework for the recognition of assets where I attempt to display as many of the 'pieces' as possible.

The existing definitions of an asset are concerned with man and his place in society

With regard to the nature of an asset, part of the agenda for those advocating change to the definition of an asset is to incorporate previously unrecognisable assets, such as internally generated brands.

The industrialised societies of the early and middle parts of the twentieth century were essentially production oriented, with supporting accounting systems which largely emphasised the effective use of tangible resources, such as capital, land and labour. Today the industrialised societies are more consumer oriented and the demand is not only for tangible assets of increasing technological sophistication, but also for the intangible assets which often support them, such as software, brands and research. One suspects that the real wealth creators in tomorrow's society will be the intellectual capacity to stay ahead of the competition or to prevent competition rather than the efficiency of some factory machine or the latest managerial philosophy? The scenario suggests a rapidly changing society, with the nature of what is capable of producing future economic benefits also changing to embrace more and more intangible assets. If correct, the existing asset definitions may become increasingly unreflective of business reality, because what is essentially the product of intellectual creativity rather than transactions or events can remain unaffected by this asset recognition trigger. This is addressed in the next chapter in some detail.

If the above scenario is correct and intangible assets, relative to tangible assets, increase in their ability to produce future economic benefits then the accounting profession is faced with a dilemma. A situation will arise where an unrecognisable intangible 'something' is actually producing sizeable income streams without the profession being able to account for it. For example, a genetically engineered bacterium may be able to convert a previously low-grade, uneconomic oil reserve into a high-grade, economically viable prospect. The bacterium, the process patent and the oil reserves are not currently regarded as assets because they do not arise from transactions or events. Indeed, the whole area of recognising and/or patenting biotechnology is fraught with ethical and legal difficulties yet it offers the potential of substantial future economic benefits. The accounting profession is aware of this problem, with a majority of respondents believing that a transaction or event can prevent recognition of an asset which is based solely on its ability to create future economic benefits. However, it has yet to result in changes in accounting recognition practices.

	Agree (%)	Net +/−
A 'transaction or event' basis for the recognition of an asset can prevent the recognition of an asset based solely upon its ability to create 'future economic benefits'	55	+51

The existing definitions of an asset facilitate choice and/or decision

The construction of a definition of an asset is a balancing act between setting asset recognition boundaries that are not too wide or too narrow. The term 'future economic benefits' can be interpreted widely so that any item that produced them could be regarded as an asset, for example, a talented human being. As the scope for varying interpretations of what constitutes future economic benefits increases, so the risk of lack of comparability between financial statements also increases as accountants selectively exercise their choices over the use of the definition. Conversely, an unduly restrictive definition of an asset, whilst it may improve comparability, runs the risk of omissions from it, such as internally created assets.

My expanded artefact-based boundary must exclude the recognition of humans as assets since by definition an artefact is something made or given shape by man; in other words, recognition of what man creates rather than man himself. Further, the artefact in question must have a legally separable identity. Thus, football stars should not appear on the balance sheet. Whilst any substitute, such as the football transfer fees capitalised by some football clubs, will have artefacts (contracts, invoices which are legally based), they are not separable from the footballer in the same way, for example, that a patent would be legally separate from the boffin who created it. If the footballer dies, logically, the transfer fees should be written off—not so with the boffin/patent situation.

There are those who would say that an expanded asset recognition boundary that excluded human assets from it, is a poor choice. I have some sympathy with that view because the reality of many service-based companies is that their main assets are human beings. Nevertheless, I have already briefly explored the accounting profession's flirtation with human resource accounting and it has been shown to lead nowhere from a measurement viewpoint. It also leads nowhere from a recognition viewpoint because humans have a happy knack of becoming intellectually or artistically 'burnt out', becoming sick or even dying. Yet what they create can live for posterity or, in the case of copyright, for at least 70 years.

The existing definitions of an asset may contain unverifiable or mistaken statements

By their nature, normative statements can be subject to disagreement as to the evidence in support of them. It follows that one has to accept the possibility of honest error in their construction. For example, some asset definitions refer to the control of 'future' economic benefits when it can be argued that the future, or indeed the past, is beyond our control. Certainly, a clear majority of respondents agreed that the *past* could not be controlled. It is possible today to control the resources which constitute an asset (IASC definition in Figure 3.1) and to have a good idea as to the effect that control has on the amount of *future* economic benefits produced, apart from unexpected events, of course. However, control is typically exercised by human beings, even with most automated systems, and they live and exercise control in the *present* only.

The definitional requirement for *future* economic benefits does not appear to sit well with a measurement basis that includes *historic* cost asset values, 'either historic cost or current value' (ASB 1999, p. 77). This was the reason for asking the question, presented earlier, whether a method of measurement (e.g. cost or cash flow) should be specified in the definition of an asset instead of the phrase 'future economic benefits'.

There are two issues here: firstly, if only for the sake of comparability there is a need to define a uniform time frame in which to account—historic, current or future—and, secondly, the choice of an appropriate measurement basis. With regard to the second issue, Aitken (1990, p. 228) maintains that 'permitting the addition and subtraction of the numbers resulting from . . . different valuation bases resembles adding or subtracting apples and oranges. The resulting numbers tell you nothing of either of the items mentioned.' With regard to the first issue, the choice of time frame may preclude certain measurement bases, for example, discounted future cash flows with a historic time frame.

Aitken (1990, p. 229) refers to five points in support of a current time frame, which may be summarised as follows:

1. It is commonly accepted that traditional financial statements refer to the past up to the present, and not to some future period.
2. The perceived progress of the business is not interpretable or verifiable beyond a dated present.
3. Whilst the users of financial statements appear to have realisable goals that require predictive information, they in fact do not. They do not because, before they can establish these goals, they need to know their present position.
4. Information that relates to future liquidity, future financial performance and gearing is of no relevance.
5. It is professionally irresponsible to use future price information, which is effectively an attempt at crystal ball gazing.

The survey question was aimed at the possible substitution of a precisely defined measurement basis for what may be regarded as an imprecisely defined 'future economic benefit'. However, this was a view that was not supported by the respondents to it. Indeed, most respondents believed the future could be controlled (only 34% agreeing that 'the future cannot be controlled' and only 16% agreeing 'it is not possible to control a future-based economic benefit'):

	Agree (%)	Net +/−
The past cannot be controlled	79	+82
The future cannot be controlled	34	−15
Control is only exercisable in present-day terms	38	+10
The UK accounting definition of an asset refers to 'future economic benefits controlled by an entity'. It is not possible to control a future-based economic benefit	16	−46

This surprising result was supported by the fact that only 38% of respondents agreed that control is only exercisable in present-day terms. Clearly there is doubt about what is meant by 'control' and the time frame over which it is viewed.

The proponents of the existing definitions of an asset seek to justify and legitimise their definitions

If the proponents of the existing asset definitions cannot be sure about their comprehensive coverage (first assumption, above), it becomes important to them to reinforce their ideas by gaining the maximum possible support for them from academics, standard-setting bodies and professionals alike. As a consequence, the possibility exists that the similarities in the existing definitions of an asset (Figure 3.1) are intended to reinforce the dominant economics-based view of assets and, in the process, neutralise potential opposition to them through the amount and importance of opinion. What matters is that the definitions are stated and accepted, with minimal dissension, as much for the benefit of those who propose them as for those who are to use them.

Most proponents of the existing definitions of an asset would not assume that their definitions contain mistakes. However, without the type of assessment carried out so far in this chapter, such proponents have no point of reference by which to judge their efforts, other than by their own version of economic reality and subjective reasoning. Under such circumstances, linguistic interpretations become problematic (e.g. defining an 'entity') and there is much credence to be gained by emulating the competition. For example, most of the existing definitions of an asset in Figure 3.1 refer to three essential features: 'future economic benefits', 'controlled', 'transactions or events'. However, the danger of this approach is that the definitions of an asset remain static or, at best, as minor refinements of a situation which is increasingly unreflective of changing economic circumstances—a case of sand built on sand. Let us consider some examples.

EXAMPLES OF THE CHANGING NATURE OF AN ASSET

Society is organised according to collectively derived institutional arrangements. Property arrangements are an important subset. These arrangements define individual rights, duties, obligations and exposures. When items become scarce, when tastes and preferences change, or when relative prices change, it follows that the old rules may no longer be applicable.

Fishing access

Consider the extension of exclusive economic zones for fishing access, such as those imposed by Iceland, a nation that is heavily dependent on fishing. It became of great importance to them to determine by agreement, or by force as a last resort, who had access to natural resources that were formerly assumed to be inexhaustible. Extending the fisheries protection zone to 200 miles created a larger zone of common property for them and, once achieved, that nation was then able to instigate institutional arrangements, such as a quota system, that would give its fishermen controlled access to the resource (Bromley 1967).

The asset element of the changing fisheries situation is demonstrated by the European Union (EU) fishing quotas. Individual quotas are assets in their own right providing the means of access to future economic benefits and capable of being sold and bought, for example, between Spanish and Scottish fishermen. Indeed, there is now an accessible market to both EU milk and fishing quotas. However, it was not until recently (ASB 1997) that the UK accounting profession was prepared to recognise such assets irrespectively of whether a quota was purchased or not. Prior to 1998 only purchased or transaction-based quotas could have been recognised as assets (quotas initially given to businesses as a result of government edicts being regarded as a free asset). They can now be recognised on the basis of a readily accessible market value (RAMV).

Websites like Yahoo!

Consider the existence of websites such as Yahoo! Whilst the market capitalisation of such website businesses is indicative of substantial future economic benefits, identifying their source is highly problematic. The internet itself is clearly a free asset. Also, whilst the subscription charge to gain access to the website is a recognisable transaction, it is hardly a recognisable asset. The real asset is the customer list of those people who, attracted by the intellectual/artistic creativity they find there, browse the website with a view to using and paying for the facilities they find there. These are assets that are currently unrecognisable by accountants because they do not arise from a transaction or event. The effect is that the current book values of these businesses are totally unreflective of their true economic worth.

Access to water holes

Even where an economy is undeveloped, the recognition of assets can change according to changing economic conditions. In many parts of pastoral Africa land is held in common for grazing purposes, with access to water holes being of critical importance. Water is the recognisable, valuable asset. However, once deep-well water pumps are operational, it is the access to the irrigated pasture that then becomes important. The ownership and protection of the land then determine one's economic prospects in this case.

Concern for environmental quality

The comparatively recent rise of concern for environmental quality (e.g. the Greenpeace organisation) is an example of how changes in tastes and preferences have brought about fundamental social change in institutional arrangements governing the use of natural resources. Changing attitudes about the importance of the natural environment (forests, air quality) and intellectual property arrangements have led to a number of legislative and judicial actions which alter the existing institutional arrangements (including property rights) with regard to the use of such natural and socially constructed resources. Presumptive property rights are constantly being challenged in the courts and in legislative assemblies throughout the world. And the process is never finished, either in the industrialised nations or in the developing industrialised countries where it is now becoming a major factor in resource management. Serious concerns for the rate of deforestation and for the effect on global warming seem certain to continue. Indeed, the Kyoto proposal for a new trade in carbon credits, buying and selling pollution rights, is but one more example of the changing nature of assets.

Summary

In summary, institutional arrangements can and will change in response to both market and extra-market pressures. The market pressures will express themselves in terms of supply chain difficulties, new contractual arrangements, price changes and also in the expression of consumer tastes and preferences. The extra-market pressures will come through pressure brought to bear in the political arena in response to market pressures. The mix between market and extra-market pressures will depend on the benefits and costs from each route.

THE NEED FOR A CHANGE TO THE DEFINITION
OF AN ASSET

The UK accounting definition of an asset (ASB 1999) is incremental to previous definitions of an asset, notably by the Financial Accounting Standards Board (FASB 1985), Solomons (1989), and the International Accounting Standards Committee (IASC 1989). The justification for this statement is that the central features of the four definitions (Figure 3.1) are similar in that they all refer to 'future economic benefits', 'controlled' usually as a 'result of past transactions' or 'events' (except Solomons re the last feature).

Their focus on the world is clearly from an economic viewpoint and in most cases is founded on the accounting premise of duality, the debtor/creditor relationship normally associated with a transaction or event. The common idea of future economic benefits is well established within the accounting community and offers a high degree of generality of representation. From a methodological viewpoint, the UK definition of an asset is qualitative in nature (ASB 1995b, Ch. 2) in that it relies on careful reasoning to establish its own credibility as a relevant and reliable way to define an asset. It is also incremental in nature in that the UK definition of an asset is an indication, intentional or otherwise, that the UK accounting profession wishes to maintain a degree of international status quo. As such, it is part of a world view informed by a Kantian/Hegelian philosophical perspective (Laughlin 1995).

It is a perspective that assumes a material world existing separately from our perceptions of it but which, to a degree, is mediated and moulded by our interpretation of it. It is a perspective where 'skeletal' generalisations exist but they can never completely capture reality, and where understanding is accessed through a mixture of structured and subjective processes. So, for example, our understanding of an asset in terms of its ability to produce 'future economic benefits' is clearly a skeletal generalisation (What is meant by economic? What is meant by benefits?) intended to portray some form of financial gain from the business use of an asset, as distinct, say, from any utilitarian benefit derived from its use in another social capacity.

Assets are a major part of the everyday material world but the accounting perception towards them is, in large part, mediated and moulded by the requirement for recognisable 'transactions or events'. This requirement structures and, at the same time, establishes a boundary to the accounting understanding of what constitutes an asset which is, indeed, subjective because it is possible to substitute an alternative structure. An alternative boundary could, for example, be established on the basis of the recognition of an asset's legally separable identity. There is also a political aspect to this 'mediation' established by the power of one party in society, the ASB, being able to dominate in the creation and acceptance of such structures and boundaries.

The accounting response to the material world in terms of asset recognition is reflected in the industrial revolutionary origins of accountants as recorders and reporters of business activity in order to ensure the proper stewardship of assets and financial propriety in commerce. However, it is possible to offer an alternative Kantian/Fichtean philosophical viewpoint (Laughlin 1995). This alternative view assumes a world whose existence is inseparable from the observer's perception of it, where generalisations cannot be assumed to exist and where understanding is specific and subjectively derived. In this view of the world there is no basis on which to judge the superiority of one interpretation over another, and therefore any attempt to do so can only be advanced and subjectively justified on the basis that it produces a 'better' view of reality. The key difference is that the

Kantian/Hegelian perspective starts with the existence of a material world. Consequently, any perception of the material world tends to be directed in the first instance towards the physical and visible aspects of it rather than to the non-physical and invisible. In contrast, from the Kantian/Fichtean perspective, the world, material or otherwise, is inseparable from the observer's perception of it. Something may be invisible or intangible in nature but, nevertheless, it may exist in the observer's perception of the world. The obvious practical contrast between the two perspectives arises in terms of the recognition of tangible assets and intangible assets, respectively.

Of course, though often synonymous with each other, one needs to be careful about confusing the 'material world' with a 'tangible world'. The Kantian/Hegelian perspective does not exclude most intangible assets, particularly where they are made material through regulation. In fact, any expenditure, whether capitalised or not, could be said to be part of the material world. The difficulty arises where, according to the Kantian/Fichtean perspective, an intangible asset is perceived to exist but has yet to enter the material world as 'mediated and moulded' by the accounting profession's view of it in terms of the recognition criteria applied to an asset. Consider, for example, the customer lists, maps, weather reports and traffic data established by some companies on the internet. To many outside the accounting profession they are part of the material world and they, either directly or indirectly, facilitate the creation of wealth. To the accountant they remain outside his/her view of the material world in terms of asset recognition and disclosure, unless someone subsequently transacts for the rights or access to them. It is this latter aspect which is addressed somewhat critically in the next chapter using brand assets as an example.

4

Transactions or events and the role of separability

Brand asset valuation companies draw on the marketing domain, where the results of their services remain largely uncontested. They then attempt to apply these services in the accounting domain, where they are contested and as a result most brand valuations are excluded from published balance sheets. This is in contrast to other external-to-accounting professional services such as property surveyors whose valuations, unlike most brand valuations, are disclosed on published balance sheets. Yet brand valuations have a role to play in the field of strategic management that can sometimes be of crucial importance to management, as for example when they are used to increase the asset base and thereby force up the bidding price in a takeover situation.

This strategic management role and a philosophy of market awareness are powerful rhetorical devices. They bind a contested service, the provision of brand valuations, to the indisputable need for information on business competitiveness, in particular to the need for more financial information on intangibles. The dominance of the accounting profession in financial matters means that in the financial accounting domain the contest is one-sided. As a result, many of the attempts outside this domain to legitimise the capitalisation and disclosure of brand assets have to assert the weaknesses of accounting (in Part One) as well as the strengths of brand asset disclosure (in Part Two). For example, Murphy (1990b) in his book *Brand Valuation: Establishing a True and Fair View*, links brand asset disclosure to the true and fair view override, thus drawing on accounting itself to legitimise the status of brand assets.

The accounting objections to existing brand valuation technologies relate principally to the issue of sufficient reliability of measurement and, by implication, to valuations in general, particularly where they arise independently of a recognisable transaction. The focus is on measurement issues which, for a profession dedicated to the accuracy of the figures it produces, is understandable. The problem with any asset valuation is that it is inevitably subjective and therefore open to manipulation and inaccuracy. The innate preference for accountants is to rely on past transaction-based values, typically a purchase or sale, because these are known with certainty, are verifiable, and the duality provided by parties to a transaction underpins most of double-entry bookkeeping. As a result, there is a tension between the desire of some accountants independently to value and disclose assets, thereby reflecting a broader picture of business reality in the figures they produce, and the restriction placed on their portrayal of that reality by the requirement for recognisable transactions or events. I will examine this tension further by reference to an asset's separable nature, that is, its 'separability'. In particular, I will look again at the accounting notion of measurement separability in more depth.

Overall so far, one is perhaps left with a view of a subject matter that is of a specialist, parochial interest. A subject matter that is best left in the accounting domain? That would be incorrect. For example, the primary duty of a board of directors is as custodians of business assets. The type of assets chosen and how well they are subsequently utilised is a major determinant of profitability and of directors' bonuses. It is therefore important in a knowledge-based economy that, in the first instance, intangible assets are separately recognised, then measured and disclosed. For it can reasonably be argued that those intangibles which are not recognised as separable assets tend not to receive the sort of managerial attention typically reserved for their tangible counterparts. The accounting response, however, has been to subsume many intangible assets within a generic goodwill figure on the balance sheet on the grounds that they cannot be measured reliably. They may have a separable identity, particularly where legal rights are present, but not in terms of determining their separable values. As a result, published financial statements as a source of information to management are in danger of becoming meaningless, particularly for knowledge-based companies.

I reject the argument that intangible assets cannot be measured reliably, firstly on the grounds that the argument is just as applicable to tangible assets. In other words, the financial picture that accountants attempt to portray is always incomplete and the issue of what should be included is simply a question of how much distortion is acceptable to the users of it. Secondly, that the recognition of a separable asset, whether tangible or intangible, is logically prior to its measurement, and measurement should not substitute for recognition according to a separable identity or nature. Finally, that the issue of separability is a crucial first step in reversing the accounting stance towards the lack of separable disclosure of intangible assets. I examine separability here in relation to brand assets but as a topic it has a broad coverage. For example, the accounting profession in the 1970s and 1980s attempted to embrace the notion of capitalising human resources, but this fell by the wayside on the grounds of unreliable measurements. Since many assets have some form of human element to them in terms of their construction or commissioning, there is a fundamental and missing 'separability' argument to be addressed first before any consideration as to measurement.

SEPARABILITY DEFINED: TWO VIEWPOINTS

Separability is defined as 'the assets or liabilities which are capable of being disposed of or discharged separately without disposing of a business of the undertaking,' as per the Companies Act 1985, schedule 4a, 9(2). It is in respect of intangible assets that the issue of separability becomes most problematic; that is, separately disposing of, or correspondingly, acquiring an asset that does not physically exist. For example, no one in their right mind would purchase goodwill separately from the other assets of a business. Yet purchased goodwill is now disclosed separately as an asset on the balance sheet even though its separable nature, according to the above definition, is highly questionable. It would appear that the accounting profession is viewing separability from a different perspective to that which would be applied by the layman from a literal interpretation of the above definition. In essence, for the accounting profession, if an intangible asset can be measured reliably, the measurement itself establishes its separability.

So, to return to the goodwill example, if a sum x is paid to acquire a business and y is the fair value of the separable net assets acquired, then $x - y$ equals purchased goodwill. Purchased goodwill is therefore measured accurately as a separately identified element of a transaction, recognised and disclosed as such on the balance sheet. The fact that $x - y$ might be negative means it is able to switch its status as an asset or as a reserve, like no other 'asset', depending on the relative proportions of x and y. One can conclude that two very different views of separability exist: one based on the accounting notion of 'measurement separability' (Napier and Power 1992) and another based on a separable nature or 'physical and/or legal separability', as per the Companies Act.

From a regulatory viewpoint, FRS10 (ASB 1997, p. 8) explains that assets and liabilities are 'identifiable' in terms of their separable nature or separability. Specifically, 'they are the assets and liabilities of an entity that are capable of being disposed of or settled separately, without disposing of a business of the entity.' The FASB (1970b) highlights the problem of separability in relation to the identification of intangible assets:

> Many kinds of intangible assets may be identified and given reasonably descriptive names, for example, patents, franchises, trademarks, and the like. Other types of intangible assets lack specific identifiability. Both identifiable and unidentifiable assets may be developed internally. Identifiable intangible assets may be acquired singly, as a part of a group of assets, or as part of an entire enterprise, but unidentifiable assets cannot be acquired singly. (APB17, para 1)

Purchased goodwill is a case in point. Likewise the AASB (1996) provides examples of unidentifiable assets such as market penetration, effective advertising, good labour relations and a superior operating team: 'Unidentifiable assets do not include assets of an intangible nature which are capable of being both individually identified and separately recognised, as may be the case with patents, licences, rights and copyrights' (AASB1013, para 5.1.1). All three regulatory bodies appear to adopt separability, that is, an asset's separable nature, as a key criterion for identification. The Institute of Chartered Accountants of New Zealand (FRSB 1999), on the other hand, states:

> Separability is not a necessary condition for identifiability since an entity may be able to identify an asset in some other way. For example, if an intangible asset is acquired with a group of assets, the transaction may involve the transfer of legal rights that enable an entity to identify the intangible asset. Similarly, if an internal project aims to create legal rights for the entity, the nature of these legal rights may assist the entity in identifying an internally generated intangible asset. Also, even if an asset generates future economic benefits only in combination with other assets, the asset is identifiable if the entity can identify the future economic benefits that will flow from the asset. (ED87, para 4.15)

It has to be said, in response, that legal rights automatically confer separability from other assets, and therefore separate identification from other assets, by virtue of those rights. Indeed, where separable identification is problematic, as with the distinction between brands and goodwill, the legal right of a related trademark may be the principal means of separable identification of a brand. Of course, much depends on whether separability is associated with the nature of an asset or what it produces in terms of future economic benefits—a measurement-focused view of separability. In the final sentence of ED87, above, identification is measurement focused in terms of future economic benefits. Thus, for example, purchased goodwill, whilst inseparable in nature from the other assets of a business, is nevertheless separable according to its existence as a measured 'difference' and in terms of the future economic benefits it is assumed to produce.

The IASC (1998) also firmly links the issue of separability with measurement:

> The identifiable assets and liabilities that are recognised ... should be those of the acquiree that existed at the date of acquisition together with any liabilities. ... They should be recognised separately as at the date of acquisition if, and only if: (a) it is

probable that any associated future economic benefits will flow to, or resources embodying economic benefits will flow from, the acquirer; and (b) a reliable measure is available of their cost or fair value. (IAS22, para 26)

See also ED87, para 5, for an identical wording of the Institute of Chartered Accountants of New Zealand viewpoint on this matter. Points (a) and (b) are measurement focused. This does not mean to say that the other regulatory bodies do not have similar measurement-based requirements but here we are investigating identification based on a separable nature rather than reliability of measurement, the former being logically prior to the latter. The only distinction to be made, in terms of separability as a fundamental feature of the nature of an asset, is that the AASB requires assets to be identified individually whereas the FASB will countenance identification singly and as a group of assets.

To repeat, outside the accounting domain, many of the attempts that seek to legitimise the capitalisation and disclosure of brand assets have to assert the weaknesses of accounting as well as the strengths of brand asset disclosure. It is not intended to advance here the strengths, if any, of various brand valuation methodologies. Rather, I seek to remain largely within the accounting domain from an information user perspective, and to examine the impact of separability on measurement issues and the weaknesses thereof. In the following section I will examine the nature of separability itself. In particular, I will address the role that 'measurement separability' appears to play in excluding valuations, such as brand valuations, from the balance sheet.

There is no precise definition of measurement separability. However, I define it here as the subsumption of the process of asset identification and recognition within asset measurement, such that asset measurement and the reliability thereof become central to accounting policy choices in respect of the separable disclosure of intangible assets. In the next section I will highlight the accounting preference for measurement separability over physical and/or legal separability on the grounds that it offers greater reliability of measurement in asset values. I will argue, however, that measurement separability tends to prejudice transaction-based measurements and that this in turn favours a transaction-based view of the balance sheet. In the section after that I address the two main approaches of asset measurement and the linkage to separability; that is, *transaction-based* measurements typically derived from purchase costs and matched (as per the matching principle) to revenues within specific periods of account, and *valuation-based* measurements as derived from independent valuations and utilising a multiplicity of methods, including cost.

By reference to practical examples within four headings, I highlight the inconsistency of transaction-based measurements and the subjectivity associated with valuation-based measurements. These methods attempt to portray two different views of the balance sheet: transaction-based measurements see it as the aggregate of an entity's separable transaction-based assets and liabilities; valuation-based measurements see it as the increase/decrease in the value of all assets and liabilities, whether recognised by transactions or not, between two balance sheet dates. I postulate that the key factor preventing the second view is what I call the 'separability initial recognition cycle', addressed in the final section of the chapter. I argue that the key feature that binds the two measurement approaches is separability, as per the Companies Act, and this should be considered as *a priori* to any measurement method applied in practice. I conclude that the accounting profession is 'hooked on the horns of a dilemma' in that neither transaction-based measurements nor valuation-based measurements are without their faults. However, it is argued that if the accounting profession is to report those, currently undisclosed, intangible assets that are an increasingly valuable feature of our knowledge-based society, it probably has little option but to embrace the subjectivity of valuation-based measurements.

THE NATURE OF SEPARABILITY: A BRIEF REVIEW OF TWO VIEWPOINTS

According to Simmonds (1994), the central test of separability can be approached in two ways. The first approach asks whether it is 'possible to define boundaries between an asset and other assets in such a way to enable it to be disposed of as a discrete asset.' Defining asset recognition boundaries inclusive of separability, however, is not without its problems—remember the earlier discussion with regard to the separability of football transfer fees. Secondly, the value of a tangible and intangible asset is, in part, determined by the use of the asset in creating wealth; that is, in combination with the expertise of those personnel controlling its productive usage. In this economic sense, very few assets are completely separable in practice.

The second question posed by Simmonds is, What will remain if the intangible asset is removed from the business? Remove the brand name of Andersen Consulting (now Accenture) from its related chartered accounting practice, and one can reasonably expect considerable financial damage to the remaining business. However, that does not mean to say that the brand is inseparable, it simply means that it is going to be expensive to replace it. The title of an *Accountancy Age* article says it all, 'Walking away from a $3bn brand' (Haigh 2000)—an expensive forced disposal, the full financial effects of which have yet to reveal themselves over time.

Simmonds shows that there are different degrees of separableness depending on where on the separability spectrum one places an intangible asset. The accounting spectrum of separability is shown in Figure 4.1.

So, for example, Simmonds locates a consumer product brand towards the separable end of the spectrum whilst a corporate brand would be located towards the inseparable end of the spectrum. However, what reinforces the concept of separability is the presence of legal rights attached to the intangible asset, whether that be by contractual relations (a transaction) or by the accounting recognition of additional legal basis such as statutory registration or, as in the case of Andersen Consulting, by court order. If an intangible asset is legally recognisable, de facto it is recognisable as a legal abstraction and its separability is not subject to degrees of separability. It simply is, or is not, legally separable. In this sense, the portrayal of a 'spectrum' with varying degrees of separability is inaccurate.

Damant (1995, p. 73) concludes that a 'precise and useful definition of separability would be that the asset in question (whether tangible or intangible) should have a separate valuation only if it has a value which is completely independent of what it is earning

Figure 4.1   The spectrum of separability

in the activity under analysis.' This view would support the valuation of intangibles by reference to evidence of recent actual transfers, but would not support valuation by reference to capitalised earnings or cash flows unless these were adopted as a surrogate of estimated market value. Although inherently attractive to accountants because of the reliance on transfers or transactions, the approach is directed toward a separable value rather than a separable nature. Archer (1994), however, is quite clear that 'the concept of separability involved is the "ontological" criterion of separate transferability, not the criterion of separate identifiability of the estimated attributable future cash flows. The latter strictly concerns the different issues of "measurability".' The subsequent reference to 'the valuation of intangibles by reference to evidence of recent actual transfer' bears some similarity to the notion of readily ascertainable market values (RAMVs), as per ASB (1997). RAMVs are also evidenced by frequent transactions or 'transfers'. The real issue, however, driving this view of separability is the desire to ground separable intangible asset values on measured transaction-based values, directly or indirectly, rather than an independent valuation, independent of transactions.

Ernst & Young (1994) refers to the definition of separability presented in companies legislation, and states:

> We do not think that separability in this sense is the real issue. Many items, not just certain intangible assets, would fail the test: other examples might include deferred tax balances, warranty provisions, pension surpluses, and so on. We suggest that the real criterion ... is whether they can be sensibly accounted for separately thereafter. This involves considerations such as whether such assets can be defined objectively and measured reliably, and in particular whether it is possible to identify when their benefits have expired so that they should be expensed in the profit and loss account.

Separability is here again related to the reliability of measurement of an asset rather than to its separable nature as an asset. The ability instead to 'sensibly account' embraces the idea of capitalising as an asset deferred items of mainly revenue expenditure, such as tax balances and warranties, whose separable nature as an asset is doubtful. It effectively highlights the dominance of transactions/transfers and the matching principle in the recognition of these 'assets' such that the balance sheet is used to 'park' such expenditures until they can be matched or consumed in the appropriate subsequent periods of account within the profit and loss account (see capitalised revenue expenses on p. 45).

So far, all that has been advanced is a necessary examination of the two aforementioned views towards separability. An important question that arises from this examination is, Why do most accountants rely on measurement separability, which initially tends to depend on a transaction-based cost, rather than physical or legal separability accompanied by an independent valuation? I will now attempt to answer it.

THE ACCOUNTING PREFERENCE FOR MEASUREMENT SEPARABILITY

Firstly, one obvious consideration in response to the above question is the absence of physical properties in the intangible asset recognition process thus necessitating, from the accounting viewpoint, the substitution of measurement for recognition. In effect, the prima facie case is that a physical and/or legal separability approach is an inappropriate basis for recognition of non-physical or intangible assets. However, I would refer the reader to the dog analogy (Chapter 1) as an effective counter-argument to this situation. For the accounting profession, if one can separately measure the intangible item, it becomes separately recognisable, even if there are some doubts about its separable nature as an asset—consider the earlier $x - y$ goodwill example. The accounting approach is supported by the UK accounting definition of an asset as 'rights or other access to future economic benefit' (ASB 1999), rather than rights or other access to the identified resources that may or may not produce future economic benefits.

There are those who believe that it is unnecessary to define and thereby separately recognise an asset prior to measurement, particularly in respect of goodwill and brands where the identification of an intangible nature and/or resource is highly problematic. For example, Weetman (1989) argues that an asset can be identified in terms of expected cash flows (a measurement) and that it may be sufficient to identify it in such terms rather than in terms of resources: 'This is because, ultimately, it might be found that equating an asset with a resource would merely shift the problem along one stage, so that the need to define a resource would replace the need to define an asset.' However, this overlooks the resource that is often common to most tangibles and intangibles alike, namely, legally established rights to future economic benefits. Whilst acknowledging that 'rights or other access to future economic benefits' do not necessarily need to be legally determined for recognition of an asset, the advantage of this approach over non-legal approaches is that legal rights automatically confer on an intangible asset a legally separable nature; that is, a separable nature according to the Companies Act definition of it, separately of any measurement of its worth. So, in the case of brands, separability is maintained by statutory registration of its related trademark, or by a successful civil action in 'passing off' (a tort), and these rights can be disposed of separately, if necessary.

Secondly, accountants have shown themselves willing to embrace all types of measurement method on the balance sheet. However, this is usually subsequent to the transaction-based cost determined by the transaction-based 'initial recognition process' of something as an asset. It is centred on the requirement for 'sufficient evidence' as to the existence of an asset and 'sufficient reliability' in its measurement (ASB 1999), both of which are secured by a transaction where the item, date and amount are usually known with a reasonable degree of certainty. Where an intangible asset has a legally separable identity there can be little doubt that there is 'sufficient evidence' for its existence despite the lack of physical properties. In this sense, accountants would probably have few problems in embracing the notion of 'physical and/or legal separability'.

It is in respect of the 'sufficient reliability' of a measurement criterion that the problems arise. Measurement is typically established by reference to a transaction cost. At the moment when a transaction occurs, the asset's original cost and market value are normally one and the same thing for that asset. However, after that moment, the original cost becomes a historic cost and the market value is subject to the vagaries of the marketplace. That is, value can be determined by a multiplicity of means such as entry prices (replacement values), exit prices (realisable values), current market prices, earnings-related prices (economic values), etc. This is one of the attractions of transaction-based cost. Initially there is no difference between cost and market value. A transaction-based cost portrays perhaps the 'true worth' of an asset at that moment. Beyond that moment the true worth, however it may be defined, has to rely on valuation-based methods such as those referred to previously. Of course, once valuations are embraced, the 'sufficient reliability' criterion becomes debatable except, to repeat, where cost and valuation are the same at the moment where a transaction occurs.

THE DOMINANCE OF TRANSACTION-BASED MEASUREMENT

A transaction for the purchase of a brand asset establishes a recognisable, often legally recognisable, entity, date and amount; for example, the £40 million purchase for the use of the Rolls-Royce brand name by BMW motor cars in 1998. In contrast, whilst an internally created brand asset is a recognisable entity, often legally recognisable through a trademark, the date and cost of creating the internally created brand asset may be indistinguishable from the totality of the transaction costs of the business. So, with regard to the Rolls-Royce example, the brand value remained internally created and unrecognisable as an asset until it was subject to a transaction for its purchase and, at that point, its existence, date and amount (in millions of pounds) became recognisable. Already there was sufficient legal evidence for its existence and there was some evidence of its ability to produce future economic benefits, otherwise BMW would not have purchased it alone. However, until it *was* purchased, its initial recognition (ASB 1999, pp. 68–70) as an asset was based on largely unidentifiable or missing transactions or events which, consequently, could not be measured accurately.

Figure 4.2 shows a process chart for the UK accounting definition of an asset. The left-hand branch refers to reliability of transaction-based measurement for an asset; the right-hand branch addresses the recognition of other relevant assets, inclusive of internally created assets, arising outside the scope of transactions or events. The transaction-based recognition of the Rolls-Royce brand would have followed the left-hand branch. However, such recognition is restrictive in the sense that the Rolls-Royce brand existed before it was subsequently purchased and was therefore 'relevant' in terms of its ability to contribute to future economic benefits before as well as after its purchase by BMW, in the right-hand branch. A transaction simultaneously creates a *recognisable* entity and a *measured* amount but it appears to preclude brand asset recognition arising outside this context; for example, recognition of an asset based on its nature and ability to produce future economic benefits, irrespective of transactions or events. Of course, this would not simultaneously establish the measured amount, but that would not preclude an independent brand valuation subsequently taking place. In respect of Rolls-Royce the transaction-based amount was viewed by some commentators as 'on the cheap' (Lex column, *Financial Times*, 29 July 98, p. 26). It is a moot point as to whether the transaction-based amount of £40 million, or an independent valuation, would represent a more accurate view of its worth. The point here is that the asset recognition boundary raised by transactions or events appears to be both robust and restrictive.

For accountants, one can see the attraction of a transaction-based approach to asset recognition and measurement but how is it linked to the notion of separability? Physical and/or legal separability addresses the nature of an asset and it therefore does not prejudice any particular measurement method subsequently applied to the asset recognised in this manner. That means the valuation does not necessarily need to arise from a transaction. Measurement separability, on the other hand, implies that if we can measure the intangible then the question of whether or not we can identify it as an asset is pre-empted. We have identified it by virtue of measuring (Napier and Power 1992). According to Napier and Power, measurement separability—like physical and legal separability—does not prejudice any particular measurement method. However, whichever method is applied, the stream of future economic benefits from one asset must be capable of being identified separately from the future economic benefits arising from the other assets within a business.

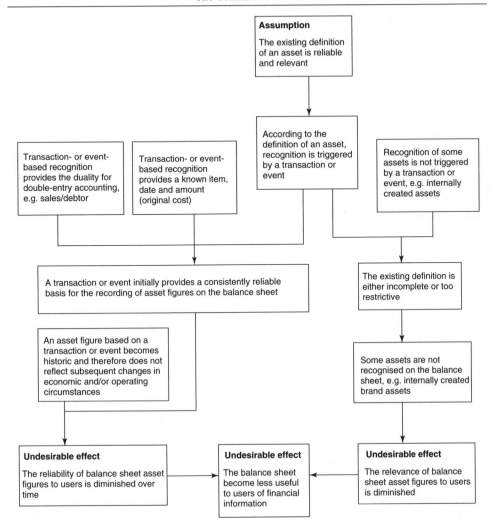

Figure 4.2 Process chart for the recognition of assets

With transaction-based asset recognition, the future economic benefit is measured at cost and it is usually 'straightforward' separately to identify the cost of one asset, or one asset from other assets, even if this requires some degree of allocation, such as that associated with a fair valuation exercise (ASB 1994). Also there is sometimes no need for a transaction actually to take place, providing there is evidence of a readily ascertainable market value (RAMV), as evidenced by numerous transactions related to assets of the same type as the asset being measured (ASB 1997). However, the contentious area is where cost/value is not determined, directly or indirectly, by reference to a transaction. In particular, where discounted cash flow techniques are used in pursuit of an economic valuation such as those so often used in the creation of brand valuations. Barwise *et al.* (1989), for example, argue that 'there is no objective way of separating a brand's incremental profit or cash flow from that of the rest of the business.'

Napier and Power (1992, p. 88) argue that 'measurement separability goes further by effectively collapsing all three stages of identification, recognition and measurement into one. In other words, if we can measure the resource in an acceptable manner, then it is difficult to resist the identification of the resource as an asset and its consequent recognition in financial statements.' The key point here is to define an 'acceptable manner'. It appears that transaction-based methods are 'acceptable' whilst valuation-based methods are less so. For example, there is no support for common brand valuation approaches, such as brand contribution methods, because of the difficulty of separating the earnings of the intangible asset to be valued from the earnings of the other assets. They argue that the whole family of brand contribution methods stands or falls on the issue of whether the use of such residual approaches can in fact dichotomise the economic benefits attributable to a business, business segment or product into those attributable to the intangible and those attributable to other assets or to a baseline unbranded product. Napier and Power also question the Arthur Andersen (1992) report, which is largely supportive of brand valuations:

> We have already alluded to an underlying circularity in the description of various valu-
> ation methods; such methods are claimed to be acceptable because separate identifica-
> tion is possible, but we argue that such methods determine, rather than depend upon,
> separability. Because of this apparent circularity, the acceptability of such methods
> cannot be determined simply by appeals to the idea of separability, because this idea
> is not independent of measurement. (Napier and Power 1992, p. 90)

However, this 'measurement only' view is perhaps unbalanced because, regardless of the reliability of the calculative technologies underpinning brand valuations, their legally separable nature is assured by legally enforceable rights; consequently, there is no 'apparent circularity'. They state that there are no criteria of identification which are independent of the measurement, but the definition of a brand asset presented later on in this book would indicate otherwise. Indeed, it almost seems that at the heart of 'measurement separability' is actually the requirement for 'sufficient reliability' of measurement. If true, and despite earlier comments to the contrary, measurement separability would also seem to prejudice transaction-based approaches because the measurement is initially deemed to be more reliable than valuation approaches.

To summarise, a physicalist and/or legalistist approach to separability initially recognises the separable nature, rather than the value of a tangible or intangible asset, recognition being logically prior to measurement. Ideally, such recognition should be based on a definition. The definition should recognise that the asset in question is separable from the human capital which created it and that it can, if necessary, be transferred to a third party independently of any other asset within a business. Measurement is not constrained by the need to recognise transaction-based values. On the other hand, measurement separability is largely unaffected by definitions of intangible assets, by their capability of separate disposal or by any attachment to human capital. If some intangible asset has worth, and the income streams from it can separately and accurately be recognised, then it is recognisable as an asset by virtue of what has been measured. Transaction-based measurements rather than valuation-based measurements are apparently preferred, though not excluded, because of the greater reliability of measurement associated with initial recognition of such assets. This, in turn, raises some interesting general questions about the role of measurements within accounting; in particular, whether the balance sheet should present entirely transaction- or event-based assets, or whether it should also embrace non-transaction-based valuations, and if the latter, whether such valuations should initially be grounded on transaction-based costs. According to Davies and Davies (1994):

> During the last twenty years a paradigm has become prevalent which gives primacy to the balance sheet. This practice was in part a reaction to high rates of inflation. The intention was to enable the balance sheet to reflect the 'true' value of an organisation, a curiously metaphysical idea in so humdrum a subject. The theory was that provided assets and liabilities could be identified and valued at the beginning and end of the accounting period, the profit must be the difference between the opening and closing net assets. Naturally, adjustments would be necessary for fresh injections of capital and payment of dividends. Criteria were established for including items in the balance sheet irrespective of transactions. Assets were generally defined in these systems as 'rights or other access to future economic benefits.'
>
> The value of these assets was to be derived from such bases as current cost, discounted future cash flow and current market price. This system introduced discretion and judgement. Preparers of accounts welcomed and soon used this freedom to create assets. Financial weakness in the balance sheet could be rectified and profit increased. Charges for diminution in value could be averted. The whole goodwill, brands and intangible assets controversy is inextricably linked to this system of reasoning. The result has been and is a muddle. Indeed, the present difficulties of the ASB are due to the balance sheet paradigm, which is fatally flawed both in principle and practice.

Let us examine this assertion further by reference to the impact that the two stated views on separability can have on the content of the balance sheet.

VALUATIONS VERSUS TRANSACTIONS/MATCHING

The dominance of transaction- or event-based measurements in the recognition of assets is deeply rooted in current accounting practice (the left-hand branch of Figure 4.2). To understand it, one needs to consider the difficulties of the measurement process itself and then in relation to the ontological security derived by accountants from their reliance on recognisable and verifiable transactions or events. The measurement process is underpinned by the accounting postulate that the unit of measure is money. It is assumed to be a relatively stable unit and it is the metric that is used as a representative proxy of economic reality for a business entity. Let us consider this statement.

Firstly, from an accounting viewpoint, monetary stability depends on whether, for example, it is representative of general purchasing power or simply units of money. The measured amount established by a transaction or event, say a purchase, is usually representative of units of money and also units of purchasing power at the date of purchase. Beyond that date the original transaction cost becomes historic cost and very often it subsequently becomes unrepresentative of general purchasing power due, for example, to the effects of inflation/deflation and holding gains/losses. However, the accounting profession is very clear that accounting measurements are not representative of purchasing power. Koeppen (1988), in referring to the US Financial Accounting Standards Board (FASB 1984) recognition criteria, states that 'the monetary unit or measurement scale ... is nominal dollars. And unless inflation escalates dramatically, nominal dollars will continue to be used for accounting measures.'

Similarly, implicit to the ASB's determination of what mix of historic cost and current value should be used (ASB 1999, technical supplement, p. 31) is the tacit acceptance of nominal sterling measurements. Ad hoc remeasurements (*ibid.*, p. 32) attempt to update historic cost values to current values in order to bridge some of the gap between units of money and their equivalent units of purchasing power. However, the gap is never bridged completely and previous comparable attempts to bridge it, for example, SSAP16 on current cost accounting (ASC 1980) were unsuccessful and subsequently withdrawn. In contrast, Chambers (1991, p. 15) maintains that 'the inputs and outputs of accounting are not "just numbers" nor "just numbers of money units", required to satisfy no other rules than the calculus of numbers. Dated amounts of general purchasing power are what commerce and finance are about.'

It is against this troubled background that intangible asset and brand valuation companies advance their case for the inclusion of intangible asset and brand valuations on the balance sheet, mostly independently of transactions or events and of the measurement established thereby. At the same time they would undoubtedly argue that it produces a 'better picture' of economic reality (a Kantian/Fichtean perspective) than that portrayed by the accounting profession using its approach to the measurement process, as discussed earlier. It is uncertain whether disclosed brand values are truly representative of general purchasing power or of some other measured view of economic reality. It is a problem that is endemic to all brand valuation technologies. To the brand valuer it probably does not matter as long as he or she can argue that a 'better picture' of economic reality is created by the inclusion of brand assets on the balance sheet. For example, using commercial realism and the current mishmash of accounting measurement bases gives a justification for one more measurement method, albeit that this usually arises from outside the accountancy profession. In contrast, to the accountant, the desire to link the recognition and disclosure of brand assets to transactions or events is sufficiently strong that brand values are nearly always extracted from the purchased goodwill arising from the transaction for the acquisition of a business. It can reasonably be argued that the linkage of brand values to purchased goodwill is probably due more to the latter's transaction-based existence and amount rather than to any conceptual linkage, particularly if it can be shown that purchased goodwill is not an asset at all.

According to Chambers (1991, p. 3), the 'neglect of the laws that govern operations on money amounts lies at the heart of all the disputed features of accounting and much of the argument about alternative systems or styles of accounting.' So it remains today, because the unit-of-measure postulate in accounting is founded on what is already accepted as logical, rather than being derived from any common accounting theory or law. There is no doubt that, as with the legal system, any common accounting theory or law would throw up practical inconsistencies, such as those presented here in respect of transaction- or event-based measurement. The point is that once inconsistencies are exposed, they might lead to some revision in the accounting theory or law, and then in practice.

According to Willett (1987, p. 160), 'there is a very general question about the nature of accounting which must be answered in any theory of accounting measurement. Is accounting measurement a process requiring the valuation of a firm's resources at different points in time, or is it concerned with the aggregation of transaction costs during an interval of time?' Proponents of the *valuations* method, perhaps, would include Sterling (1970): 'Income is the difference between wealth at two points in time plus consumption during the period.' Proponents of the *transactions* method treat the income concept as basic and they, perhaps, would include notable academics such as Ijiri (1965) and Mattessich (1964). It is interesting to note that the UK accounting definition of 'asset' (ASB 1999,

p. 50) is a composite of the valuation and transaction methods. The term 'future economic benefits' is broad enough to allow any measurement method whereas the measurement initially determined by 'transactions or events' is usually the original or historic cost. In this regard, Davies and Davies (1994) offer the following incisive comment:

> Let us assume a company mistakenly buys polluted land, which can never be rented, occupied or sold. According to the future economic benefits definition of an asset, the company does not have an asset, because although the company owns the land, no future economic benefit can be derived. Such reasoning offends common sense. In fact, an asset (the land) is owned by the enterprise, but the cost needs to be fully provided in the accounts. On the other hand, according to the ASB's definition of an asset, any expenditure which has future economic value is an asset. By this definition, the following are assets: money spent obtaining a covenant not to compete, advertising or promotional expenses. ... None of the preceding items are currently recognised as assets by any accounting standard body in the world.

A central problem associated with a 'valuations' approach is the concept of wealth, which is a concept that is difficult to pin down. The brand valuer would undoubtedly argue that the accounting view of the wealth of a business should necessarily be inclusive of intangibles. Brand asset disclosures, for example, are usually inclusive of *valuations* and exclusive of *transactions*, other than in respect of their linkage to the transaction for purchased goodwill. However, Willett (1987, p. 161) argues, in respect of applying valuation concepts to accounting measurement, that 'unless very stringent conditions are imposed on the analysis, it is impossible to produce unique number assignments even in principle.' With regard to brand asset valuations, in particular, the problem is compounded when the related units of measure are constructed from a composite of marketing and financial metrics, albeit that the final brand valuation is financial in nature.

For accountants, it is important that the unit of measure as represented by money can be added or subtracted and ordered in the usual way. However, brand valuations tend not to be additive; that is, they are one-off events at a particular moment and the only way to establish additions or subtractions to wealth over time would be to repeat the brand valuation periodically using the same method. Similarly, Whittington (1974, p. 100) argues that the 'decisions to hold, sell or buy assets will be based upon a comparison of values arising from alternative courses of action. It follows that no single valuation of an asset is relevant to decision making, at least two values are necessary in order to make a comparison.' With regard to a valuation approach, the accountant has to know the circumstances under which this occurs so that there is a common understanding of what is happening when measured additions or subtractions take place, particularly at different time intervals. In particular, given the fickle nature of brand assets, the 'circumstances' would probably need to be regulated in some way to achieve the degree of 'common understanding' for comparative financial reporting purposes. Even then, assuming there is no apparent change in measurable brand-related circumstances between two times, the valuations approach would still be subject to the vagaries of an imperfect market where market-related data is used in the brand valuation. In fact, it is accepted that the presence of imperfect or incomplete markets leads to the measurement of market values and economic income that are entirely subjective (Beaver 1981). Further, with regard to benchmarking any brand valuation by reference to a brand asset market alone, it could reasonably be regarded as, at best, 'thin', 'volatile' and therefore unreliable.

There is a link between economic valuations and the concept of utility, which in the context of financial statements relates to user utility. However, this linkage is indirect in that utility is not an extensive attribute, in the same way that money is an extensive attribute. That is, units of utility are not additive in the same way that money, per se, is additive because any measurement of utility typically has to be postulated in the context of individual consumer behaviour. Willett (1988, p. 79), however, states that

> any notion that physical things have a subjective utility value to the preparer or the user of accounts is avoided in transactions theory. . . . Debts are created and resources exchanged over time in transactions-theory and that is the basis of everything in the system of measurement.

Gambling (1971, p. 3), for example, argues that

> so long as accounting is used for its original purpose of providing control over legally created assets, such as debtors, creditors, and cash, no problems arise over the interpretation of the output. When accounting records are extended to reflect the economic well-being of the enterprise, however, disputes arise as to the true measuring of the contents of its accounting system. This is almost certainly because in its origin, accounting was concerned solely with this element of control over legal rights.

Grinyer (1994, p. 156) argues that transaction/matching-based balance sheets

> do not show the value of the assets owned by the business, merely, the previous investments outlays which have not yet been matched against expected benefits. . . . One should, then never criticise matching based balance sheets for failing to show the worth of assets. They do not claim to do so!

In contrast, valuation-based methods are entirely different in conception to 'matching-based' approaches. Essentially they identify profit as the change in the worth of the business between two times. Consequently, they require procedures for the valuation of the business. Such procedures inevitably involve assumptions, because the value of businesses will differ depending on the prevailing circumstances. Similar to the Davies and Davies comment, Grinyer (1994, p. 158) states:

> Only confusion can, however, result if one attempts to mix matching-based allocation concepts with valuation-based concepts of adequate disclosure of worth. Resulting figures of profit would then have no definable meaning.

Unfortunately, the mixing of matching- and valuation-based concepts seems to underlie most of the ASB's recent Statement of Principles (ASB 1999, technical supplement, pp. 21–22; ASB 1997). For example, the current goodwill accounting method has two elements to it: capitalisation/amortisation and capitalisation/impairment review, the former being reasonably consistent with the matching concept and existing transaction-based accounting practice, the latter with a valuation-based approach where discounting techniques are applied in what is known as 'ceiling tests'.

To summarise, what is emerging from the above assessment is that, whilst there is a strong adherence to transaction-based measurements, there is also a recognition that they present a limited view of business reality. Further, whilst valuations provide a more up-to-date picture of business reality, there is a reluctance to embrace valuations independently of the transaction-based measurement established at the initial recognition stage of an asset. The result is a hybrid balance sheet offering a multiplicity of measurement methods, whether transaction based or valuation based. Let us consider how the mix of transaction-based and valuation-based measurements can arise in practice by reference to a number of examples under four headings. In most cases the accounting preference for transaction-based measurements is clear.

Unrecognised intangible assets

Unrecognised intangible assets are intangible assets that exist in reality but do not comply with the UK accounting definition of an asset. These are assets which, in the main, are internally created by a business; that is, they are not the result of recognisable transactions or events. For example, Grand Metropolitan plc (now part of Diageo plc) recognised and capitalised the transaction-based or purchased Burger King brand as an asset whilst excluding the home-grown Croft brand from the assets on its balance sheet. If both brands are capable of creating future economic benefits then, prima facie, both should be regarded as assets. It is perhaps unnecessarily restrictive to exclude one of them from the balance sheet because it is not the result of recognisable transactions or events, and thus would require an independent valuation for such inclusion.

Capitalised revenue expenses

Capitalised revenue expenses are items of expenditure normally appearing in the profit and loss account but which are deferred and capitalised instead. No attempt is made to ascertain whether by nature the expenditure is an asset or not. Typically, such expenditure relates to business start-ups such as the staff costs associated with commissioning a new building or piece of equipment. For example, Carlton Communications plc capitalises pre-transmission revenue expenditure (excluding programming) in respect of the Television Division, which is deferred and charged to profit and loss over the initial licence period. Other examples include Securicor plc, which capitalises certain development and pre-operational costs (establishing new branches, services and products) that it acknowledges as being 'mainly of a revenue nature.' Similarly, Ladbroke plc (now Hilton Group plc), in its accounting policies, refers to the deferral of pre-operational expenses on new hotel developments, to be depreciated over five years. Even if one assumed, for example, that pre-operational costs were capable of producing future economic benefits, their appropriating capabilities are at best indirect; that is, they are linked to the other assets of a business.

The justification for deferring expenditure is usually the matching concept, which dominates irrespective of whether or not by nature the expenditure is an asset. In effect, the balance sheet becomes a dumping ground for expenses which if they had been charged in 'one hit' to the profit and loss account may have led to unacceptable fluctuations in reported annual profit figures. Instead, companies amortise the expenditure over a number of years.

Capitalised substitute assets

Capitalised substitute assets arise where the wrong 'asset' is capitalised. For example, ICL plc capitalises the costs of producing software products once a detailed program design or working model has been established. It is likely that the majority of such costs comprise the aggregate of thousands of individual transactions for the use of labour, in the creation of software products. Similarly, Great Universal Stores plc capitalised database information on the basis of 'data purchase and data capture costs of internally developed databases.' It is possible that some of the more gifted computer staff could be regarded as human assets in their own right, but this is not the issue here. The issue is that, in the main, labour costs rather than the future economic benefits from the software program or information databases themselves are being capitalised, the former being transaction based and the latter requiring an independent valuation. It appears to be more important to accountants to aggregate the transaction-based cost of labour than to value independently the future economic benefits from something as potentially fickle and short-lived as a software program. (Note also the earlier comments on the difference between human capital and intellectual capital.)

Pseudo-assets

Pseudo-assets are those 'assets' which, simply, are not assets. The accounting policies of BP plc refer to the charging 'against income' or classifying as an 'intangible asset' or transferring to 'tangible production assets' the costs of gas and oil exploration, depending on whether, respectively, they are unsuccessful or in the early stages of exploration, or successful in finding a viable mineral deposit. As a result, exploration costs exhibit the characteristics of a chameleon: they change their colour or nature according to operating circumstance. It is difficult to think of another type of 'asset' which is capable of being categorised as both intangible and tangible unless, paradoxically, exploration costs are not really assets? Exploration costs tend to be sunk costs, such as day-to-day drilling expenses, and they seldom produce future economic benefits themselves; they are simply the means to access the true source of future economic benefits, namely the mineral deposits. In contrast, Shell Transport and Trading plc charges exploration costs to income when incurred, with the exception that exploratory drilling costs are initially included in tangible fixed assets pending determination of commercial reserves. Although Shell's approach, with regard to the recognition of intangible assets, appears to be more prudent than that of BP plc, it still fails to recognise the mineral reserves as assets.

Let us summarise this section so far by reference to Table 4.1. One suspects that those who, outside the accounting domain, advance the case for the accounting recognition of brand assets would prefer a valuation-based approach to accounting, particularly brand valuers. One also suspects that they advance their case for valuations possibly in disregard for the financial measurement difficulties raised in this chapter and the wider duty that the accounting profession owes to all financial information users, and not just those who are interested in brand assets. I suggest, however, that the biggest hurdle preventing the accounting disclosure of intangible asset valuations is what I call here the 'separability initial recognition cycle' (Figure 4.3). The next section addresses this cycle and the relationship of brand asset recognition to it.

THE SEPARABILITY INITIAL RECOGNITION CYCLE

Each box in Figure 4.3 is labelled with a letter for use in the subsequent analysis. The most common manner in which an asset is separately recognised by the accounting profession is transaction based, C-E-J-R, or event based, C-E-I-P. However, the term 'events'

Table 4.1   Transaction- and valuation-based recognition and measurement

Transaction-based recognition and measurement	Valuation-based recognition and measurement
Only purchased brands are separately recognised or as an extraction from purchased goodwill. Purchase is required	Any brand, including internally created brands, can be recognised and valued independently of purchased goodwill
Capitalised revenue expenditure occurs as per the matching principle. Status as an asset is irrelevant to balance sheet disclosure	Recognition of asset status is logically prior to any valuation of it. Matching does not dictate content of balance sheet
The transaction-based cost is the asset at initial recognition stage. The cost is the asset	Valuation is not necessarily dependent on a cost established at any stage of recognition
Cost capitalisation can lead to the wrong asset being recognised and capitalised, e.g. exploration *cost* rather than the future economic benefits from mineral deposits	Asset definition inclusive of resource recognition and separability helps to distinguish assets from expenses. It identifies the asset to be valued
Measurement separability dominates in intangible asset recognition	Valuation is subsequent to intangible asset recognition. Separability is determined by nature of asset, not its measurement
Remeasurements subsequent to initial recognition rely on valuations	Consistent initial measurement and subsequent remeasurement basis

(ASB 1999) has recently been expanded to include assets K-L-M. Also the recent broadening of the existing asset recognition boundary to include those assets having a 'readily ascertainable market value' (ASB 1997) can and does occasionally embrace the recognition of assets N and O. The list of assets is not exhaustive. For example, box A refers to business assets but the list could be extended to include non-profit-making assets, as with public monuments. Most of the business asset types K to R can therefore be recognised by accountants, it is simply that their initial recognition tends to be transaction based.

So, for example, the recognition of the Rolls-Royce brand asset would have followed the C-E-D-F-K route and since S is not available, the cycle would have repeated itself until such time that the Rolls-Royce name was sold or licensed, for example to BMW in 1998. In which case it would transfer to the C-E-J-R route and would be recognised as an asset, whereas no asset was recognisable before. Yet the common feature that binds both routes is box C, the fact that the Rolls-Royce brand is separable whether that be by recognition of the intellectual or artistic property in its trademark or by a transaction. There is nothing to stop the accounting profession from respectively recognising or not recognising intangible assets on the basis of their separable nature (box C) or their inseparable nature (box B). However, the profession would probably have to accept valuations at the initial recognition stage for an asset with all the attendant subjectivity that goes with it.

The Australian Accounting Standards Board has already moved in this direction with its accounting standard AASB1037 on self-generating and regenerating assets (SGARAs); see box L. The valuation of SGARAs is to be based on net market value (para 5.2). However, there is also a requirement for an active and liquid market (para 5.3), which it shares

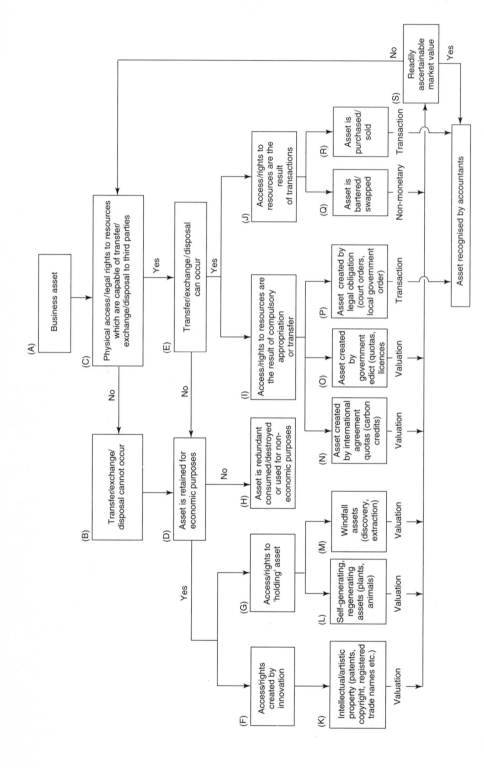

Figure 4.3 The separability initial recognition cycle

with the UK concept of a readily ascertainable market value (box S). It would appear that the overriding requirement is not measurement separability so much as measurement reliability. In accepting valuations at the initial recognition stage of an asset, the circularity of the separability initial recognition cycle, presented in Figure 4.3, would be broken and many more intangible assets could be recognised as assets on the balance sheet.

SUMMARY

I have presented an argument that asset recognition is logically prior to measurement and that intangibility does not prevent the operation of that logic, albeit that because of the lack of physical attributes, intangible asset recognition would necessarily occur on the basis of a legally separable identity. Such a basis is entirely consistent with the Companies Act 1985 definition of separability, which is largely unrelated to the accounting notion of measurement separability in that measurement is separate from and subsequent to the recognition of a physical and/or legally separable nature. Thus, in applying this logic, asset measurement does not necessarily need to occur at the same time that recognition takes place, as it does with a transaction. I have explored the subjectivity of valuations in general and of brand valuations in particular. However, I have also shown some of the practical weaknesses of a transaction-based approach.

I conclude that the accounting profession is caught on the 'horns of a dilemma'. It can retreat to a pure transaction-based approach and perpetuate the exclusion from the balance sheet of those intangibles not caught by the existing asset recognition boundary. Alternatively, it can perpetuate the current hybrid of only recognising transaction-based assets at the initial recognition stage of an asset, and then subsequently allowing revaluations to occur to these assets alone. Finally, it can embrace a valuation-based approach from the outset of the asset recognition process on the basis of a physical and/or legally separable identity requiring a regular assessment of its worth. This chapter has shown that none of these approaches is without its problems. However, the current hybrid approach is perhaps the worst approach to adopt because, whilst it offers the flexibility to mix measurement methods and related time frames (historic, current and future), it lacks a single coherent conceptual basis grounded firmly on transaction-based or valuation-based measurement. Thus, for example, one can capitalise purchased patents and capitalise those patents allowable under SSAP13 (ASC 1989a), whilst at the same time subsuming them within purchased goodwill under FRS10 and expensing them where they are internally created by a business. It must surely leave the user of financial statements totally perplexed as to their usefulness, at least for comparative purposes.

A transaction-based approach is a tried, tested and verifiable approach to asset recognition and measurement but it now appears that it is unable to capture enough intangible assets to portray an acceptable picture of business reality, particularly for those high-tech, research-led companies so characteristic of today's business climate. Nevertheless, it is a legitimate stance to adopt, providing users know the limitation of this approach. In contrast, the accounting profession can attempt to portray a broader picture of business by reference to a greater use of valuations in the reporting process. In so doing, it would address the criticisms of many leading firms of chartered accountants, and those outside the profession, who urge a move towards the separable recognition of intangibles using valuation-based measurement methods. Such an approach would necessitate codification and regulation of valuation methods so as to reduce the scope for subjectivity in measurements. Whether the accounting profession chooses to adopt such an approach is essentially a political decision, but what this chapter highlights is the importance of separability in that decision-making process.

5

The impact of FRS10 on the accounting recognition of intangible assets

In August 1988 Grand Metropolitan (now part of Diageo) announced the capitalisation of brand names worth £588 million. The debate which followed this decision became a sideshow of a long-standing goodwill debate, Should goodwill be written off to reserves or capitalised as an asset on the balance sheet, inclusive or exclusive of brands? This debate would probably have remained within the purview of the accounting profession were it not for the more contentious issue of internally created brands. This issue came to prominence in September 1988 when Ranks Hovis McDougall plc (now part of Tomkins plc) announced the capitalisation of some internally created brands, 'acquired or otherwise'. The effect, in part, was to broaden the debate to embrace the issue of the usefulness of the balance sheet in assessing the underlying strength of a business, from a user perspective. A key feature of that 'underlying strength' was, and still is, the value to a business of the income generated by intangible assets. Rumblings about existing goodwill accounting 'write-off' practices found a new voice through the capitalisation of brands as assets extracted from purchased goodwill.

The Accounting Standards Committee (ASC) in January 1989 promptly issued Technical Release 738 to discourage the capitalisation of brands. This was followed some months later by a joint ICAEW/London Business School report, *Accounting for Brands* (Barwise *et al*. 1989), which also discouraged their capitalisation (Sherer 1991). Later still, in May 1990, the Accounting Standards Committee (ASC 1990) in ED52, *Accounting for Intangible Assets*, advised that 'brands are to be subsumed within goodwill'. From this point onwards the accounting profession's views became entrenched into two camps: those few finance directors who were prepared to capitalise brands, as extracted from purchased goodwill, and the vast majority of companies who continued to adopt the 'establishment' view of non-recognition of brands as assets.

For the majority of companies, brands were, and still are, inextricably linked to purchased goodwill and this is reflected in the accounting literature. Indeed, ED52 (p. 10) tended to regard them as inseparable: 'the term brand is used to describe what is generally regarded for accounting purposes as goodwill, that is, a combination of factors which is expected to produce enhanced earnings in the future.' Contrast this view with the legally separable view of brands as expressed in this book, a view that is largely unrelated to goodwill.

Much of the debate on accounting for intangibles then turned upon:

- The merits of various goodwill accounting methods. Grinyer *et al*. (1990, p. 223), for example, argued that capitalisation and amortisation of goodwill was preferable to the then dominant SSAP22 (ASC 1989b) method of writing off goodwill on the grounds of 'improving current practice'.
- The motivations for the capitalisation of intangibles, such as reduced gearing, assisting in future borrowing decisions or defensive information in the face of a takeover (Egginton 1990, p. 196). Wines and Ferguson (1993, p. 90), for example, indicate that

companies had capitalised identifiable intangibles from goodwill to reduce the impact on profits of amortisation charges. Also Grinyer *et al.* (1991, p. 51) found that the relative proportions of purchase price assigned to separable net assets and to goodwill were affected, among other things, by gearing levels.

- The growth and market effects of purchased goodwill, e.g. Hodgson *et al.* (1993), Chauvin and Hirschey (1994), McCarthy and Schneider (1995), Jennings *et al.* (1996) and Higson (1998).

In 1992 two important documents were published: *Goodwill and Other Intangibles* by Arnold *et al.* and *The Valuation of Intangible Assets* by Arthur Andersen. Arnold *et al.* proposed the decomposition of goodwill into three items: separable intangibles, present value of profits arising from market imperfections, and over- and underpayments (Arnold *et al.* 1992, p. 68). Lee (1993, p. 82) would probably reject the decomposition stance on the grounds that 'goodwill should be accounted for as [an] integral part of the whole business entity, rather than on the problematic basis of allocation and valuation.' The Arthur Andersen publication indicated that it was sufficient to recognise such assets in terms of valuation methods, including the valuation of brands. Barwise *et al.* (1989, p. 31), however, would probably disagree with such a view: 'Even if there is some way of defining a brand as something legally separable, it may ... be impossible to find a valid (in terms of economic value) and objective way of separating its incremental profit or cash flow from that of the rest of the business.' Similarly, Napier and Power (1992, p. 94) were critical of the Arthur Andersen report as a 'lobbying document', and said that 'intangible asset research would have to reach a critical mass which is not purely a function of high quality reasoning.'

From a regulatory viewpoint, 1993 saw the issue of a discussion paper (ASB 1993) that proposed three accounting methods for each of two main stances: recognition of goodwill and intangibles as assets, and recognition of goodwill and intangibles as something to be written off. In 1995 the ASB issued a working paper (ASB 1995a) which recommended the capitalisation of goodwill, and this was followed for the first time in the ASB's history by public hearings on the issue. In 1996 the ASB issued FRED12 on goodwill and intangible assets (ASB 1996) followed, in 1997, by FRS10 on the same subject (ASB 1997). By this stage, the accounting profession had fully embraced the notion of goodwill as an asset, to be amortised over 20 years unless the presumption as to its life was rebutted to the contrary.

Financial Reporting Standard 10 (FRS10) on goodwill and intangible assets (ASB 1997) does not specifically address the recognition of brand assets, but it does refer, among other things, to the following in respect of intangibles:

- 'An intangible asset purchased separately from a business should be capitalised at cost' (para 9).
- 'An intangible asset acquired as part of the acquisition of a business should be capitalised separately from goodwill if its value can be measured reliably on initial recognition' (para 10). The key here, in respect of brand assets, is whether or not they can be measured with 'sufficient reliability'.
- 'An internally developed intangible asset may be capitalised only if it has a readily ascertainable market value' (para 14). It is doubtful whether a readily ascertainable market value (RAMV) exists for brands because the market is, at best, thin and volatile (ASB 1997, p. 14). According to Kennedy (1998), 'we don't expect to see very many of

them and their accounting is not really what this standard is all about. Quite difficult to find examples but EU milk quotas and airport landing slots appear to fit the category.'

- 'If its value cannot be measured reliably, an intangible asset purchased as part of the acquisition of a business should be subsumed within the amount of the purchase price attributed to goodwill' (para 13). This represents the overwhelming majority of accounting practice in the UK at the moment.

An interesting feature of these items is that intangible asset 'recognition' is typically expressed in terms of a 'measurement' (at cost, fair value or RAMV). No attempt is made to recognise the nature of intangible assets, albeit that this is somewhat problematic. I address that situation in the next chapter.

From an accounting viewpoint, it is much easier to dump all intangibles under the heading of purchased goodwill and amortise them, than it is to separately disclose them. There is no need to justify their separate disclosure and little incentive to value them independently of the known transaction-based cost of purchased goodwill. If anyone asks what goodwill is, accountants can point to a definition which explains that it is a 'difference'. Everyone can then see how it is determined but everyone is still none the wiser as to what it is. Everyone can see that it has a transaction-based cost, and that there are empirical studies which show there is something there that produces wealth. Therefore it must be an asset. Rubbish. Clearly there is something over and above the tangible assets of a business which may be producing wealth, but to disclose it as goodwill is akin to capitalising a bag of shopping. Everyone wants to look inside to see what can be consumed. Wouldn't it be a shock if they found that the goodwill bag was empty? Now, I wanted to see whether there were companies who were prepared to take the shopping out of the bag and disclose to everyone, item by item, intangible asset by intangible asset, what they believed represented the intangible wealth creators of their business. Hence the results of a longitudinal survey.

LONGITUDINAL SURVEY

I undertook a longitudinal survey of intangible asset accounting practices for the period 1993–2000, that is five years pre FRS10 and three years post FRS10. It was a static sample of the top 227 UK PLCs by turnover, according to the Times 1000 list of companies. It has previously been presented in a summarised form in the Brand Finance Report (Brand Finance 2000) and has since then been updated. As a static sample, it has nevertheless been declining over the years due to the effect of takeovers, and so on.

The data set was chosen for two reasons: firstly, because it captured all those companies who sponsored the Arthur Andersen (1992) report into the valuation of intangible assets and, secondly, because it favoured manufacturing, leisure, communication and retail companies but excluded banks, insurance companies, investment trusts, property companies and other financial institutions. I hypothesised, rightly or wrongly, that the non-finance group of companies (99% of companies in the data set) would be likely to show a higher incidence of brand accounting practices than the finance companies. Certainly, as Tables 5.3 and 5.4 show, pre FRS10 there was an increase in the number of companies adopting brand accounting practices within the chosen sample and also an increase in the amount capitalised. It is also interesting to note that none of the above sponsors can be categorised as financial institutions, according to the *Financial Times* categories in Table 5.1. The number and type of companies contained in the data set, for 1993, are set out in Table 5.1.

Table 5.1 Data set company groupings (number of companies 1993)

Alcoholic beverages	3	Healthcare	4
Breweries, pubs and restaurants	4	Household goods	5
Building materials and merchants	17	Insurance	2
Chemicals	8	Leisure and hotels	7
Construction	11	Media	12
Distributors	10	Oil	5
Diversified industries	5	Paper, packing and printing	5
Electricity and gas	18	Pharmaceuticals	4
Electronics and electrical equipment	8	Support services	8
Engineering	34	Telecommunications	4
Extractive industries	2	Tobacco	2
Food producers	13	Transport	7
Food retailers	7	Water	6
General retailers	16	Total	227

Table 5.2 Data set movement due to takeovers and mergers, etc.

	1993	1994	1995	1996	1997	1998	1999	2000
Opening balance	227	227	225	222	210	200	188	174
Takeovers and mergers	–	(1)	(2)	(11)	(9)	(8)	(13)	(16)
Deleted (private co., dollar listing, receivership)	–	(1)	(1)	(1)	(1)	(4)	(1)	(1)
Closing balance	227	225	222	210	200	188	174	157

Within the data set, if two companies have merged or one has taken over another, then obviously only one company remains within the sample. Where, within the sample, one company has merged or has been taken over by another company outside the sample then that company is removed from the data set. Whilst this approach to data management has worked well, it does hide a number of anomalies which have been ignored in the subsequent analysis. For example, House of Fraser plc was a private company for a short while during 1994 and both Amstrad plc and ICL plc, in 1997, are significantly different companies from those of 1993 because they have since divested themselves of a large part of their computer businesses. However, it is in the nature of business that it is permanently dynamic. So, whilst I am aware of the more public and significant company-specific developments, the word 'anomalies' is probably applicable to all of the sample companies—it is simply a question of degree. Table 5.2 shows the change in the number of PLCs within the survey sample since 1993.

Table 5.3 summarises the number of companies that disclose intangible assets, including brand assets, on their balance sheets. The level of intangible disclosure remained fairly static over the period 1991–1997 but remember this is from a survey sample that has been steadily decreasing in size over the period. The only obvious counter-trend was the increase in brand asset disclosure during this period, but the numbers were still small relative to the sample size. From 1998 onwards one can see the full effect of FRS10, particularly the capitalisation of purchased goodwill. Table 5.4 takes Table 5.3 and translates it into monetary terms.

Table 5.3   Incidence of intangible asset disclosure on UK balance sheets

	1993	1994	1995	1996	1997	1998	1999	2000
Intangible assets (generic)	9	9	9	9	9	8	8	8
Goodwill assets	5	7	7	6	8	79	131	131
Brand assets	8	9	10	10	10	8	6	7
Copyright	7	8	8	7	7	5	7	6
Licences and concessions	5	4	3	3	3	4	3	7
Patents	2	2	2	2	2	2	2	1
Software and databases	2	2	2	2	4	4	2	3
Development expenditure	9	6	5	4	3	3	5	4
Exploration expenditure	7	7	7	7	7	5	5	4
Total	54	54	53	50	53	118	169	171

Table 5.4   Incidence of intangible asset disclosure (£m) on UK balance sheets

	1993	1994	1995	1996	1997	1998	1999	2000
Intangible assets	426	431	394	393	447	270	146	110
Goodwill assets	113	1 541	1 506	1 426	2 439	12 334	40 871	115 337
Brand assets	6 431	7 686	9 992	9 659	9 306	8 797	9 287	11 883
Copyright	4 794	5 209	5 123	3 874	4 061	2 270	3 455	4 671
Licences and concessions	542	578	435	496	948	514	596	1 249
Patents	62	105	98	122	165	233	289	334
Software and databases	121	142	157	152	270	579	156	271
Development expenditure	97	65	44	33	29	80	70	69
Exploration costs	6 852	6 930	8 516	7 095	5 966	510	562	599
Total (£m)	19 317	22 687	26 265	23 250	23 631	25 587	55 705	134 523
Total intangibles/TNA (%)	4.32	4.99	5.50	4.99	5.28	7.48	14.19	23.18

Most attention will be directed towards goodwill and brand assets since they are the main focus of this book. The remaining types of intangible cannot be ignored, because they have a bearing on the content of Part One and because some of the extracts presented here make reference to brands subsumed within them.

INTANGIBLE ASSETS: A GENERIC BALANCE SHEET HEADING

Intangible assets is the most problematic heading from Tables 5.1 and 5.2 because there is not enough detailed information to break it down into its constituent elements. This would be of concern to the accuracy of the analysis of brand assets if it transpired that many brand assets were hidden as part of this generic heading. For example, survey sample companies such as Boots plc disclose trademarks under this heading. However, the value of intangibles disclosed under this heading relative to total disclosed intangible asset values is small and, in percentage terms, has decreased from approximately 2.2% in 1993 to under 0.6% in 2000 after excluding the goodwill (0.08% if goodwill is included). The impact in terms of the explicit disclosure of brand assets is negligible. The most common reference, respectively, in the accounting policies and in the notes to the accounts is

Balance sheet			2000	1999
Fixed assets			£m	£m
Intangible assets	Note 10		62.3	2.2
Tangible assets	Note 11		1799.0	609.9
Investments	Note 12		141.2	1783.3
			2002.5	2395.4

Note 10: Intangible fixed assets	Purchased goodwill	Group patents, trademarks and other product rights acquired	Group total £m
Cost	26.1	59.7	85.8
Amortisation	2.1	21.4	23.5
Net book value at 31 March 2000	24.0	38.3	62.3

Brands previously acquired by Boots Healthcare International (BHI), namely Dobendan and its derivatives, and Migranin are well known and well positioned in their markets and BHI plans to improve this position. BHI concluded that these brands have an indefinite useful economic life and they are not being amortised. As a consequence an annual impairment review is being undertaken. The valuation of these brands is significantly in excess of the carrying value.

Figure 5.1   Boots plc published accounts extract

to 'other' and 'patents, trademarks and other', including variations on 'other' such as licences, know-how and product rights. As the majority of those companies making such disclosures are either directly or indirectly involved with the chemicals industry, one suspects that the bulk of the capitalised expenditure under these headings relates mainly to purchased patent rights. Sample PLCs who in 2000 disclosed under this heading are Brunel Holdings, Boots, BOC, Esso UK, Diageo, Hays, Kingfisher and Smith & Nephew. An example of this type of disclosure is shown in Figure 5.1.

PURCHASED GOODWILL

Pre FRS10

According to Statement of Standard Accounting Practice 22 (SSAP22) on goodwill and intangible assets (ASC 1989b), there are two ways of accounting for purchased goodwill. One can write it off to reserves in the year of acquisition, which is by far and away the most common practice in the UK (96–98% of the data set companies); or one can recognise it as an asset and capitalise it. Data set PLCs who, immediately prior to the implementation of FRS10, capitalised purchased goodwill are BP, Cowie, Reuters, Shorts, Shell Transport and Trading, SmithKline Beecham and 3M.

Post FRS10

With effect from 23 December 1998, all UK companies were required to capitalise purchased goodwill. This minority option under SSAP22 is now to be the only method allowable under Financial Reporting Standard 10 (ASB 1997). One of the few companies

Balance sheet		1997	1996
Fixed assets		£m	£m
Intangible assets: goodwill	Note 16	157	198
Tangible assets	Note 17	816	775
Investments	Note 18	73	53
		1046	1026

Note 16	Cost	Amortisation	NBV
Intangible assets: goodwill			
	£m	£m	£m
31 Dec 1996	464	(266)	198
Additions	10	–	10
Amortisation charged in year	–	(51)	(51)
31 Dec 1997	474	(317)	157

Prior year adjustment In 1997 the UK Accounting Standards Board issued Financial Reporting Standard 10, *Goodwill and Intangible Assets*. Reuters has implemented this Standard which requires purchased goodwill and intangible assets to be capitalised and amortised through the profit and loss account over their useful economic lives. All goodwill previously eliminated against reserves has been reinstated as an asset on the balance sheet by way of prior year adjustment and cumulative amortisation as at 31 December 1994 has been written off against the brought forward profit and loss account reserves at that date.

Figure 5.2   Reuters plc published accounts extract

to comply early with Financial Reporting Standard 10 (FRS10) in 1997 was Reuters plc. Most companies complied with FRS10 in 1998. Reuters was also one of the few companies who chose to capitalise all purchased goodwill previously written off to reserves. Most companies chose to capitalise/amortise goodwill post FRS10 only. Consider Figure 5.2.

Since there is no reserve write-off option under FRS10, it is clear that purchased goodwill asset is to become a significant feature of UK balance sheets (Tables 5.3 and 5.4).

Of the 79, 131 and 131 sample companies who, respectively, in 1998, 1999 and 2000 capitalised purchased goodwill, only 8 of them capitalised all their goodwill, past and present. In most cases the prior year capitalisation was substantial, GEC plc (now Marconi plc), for example, amounting to over £3.2 billion. The only company to adopt the FRS10 option of capitalising post FRS7 goodwill was Pilkington plc, that is, from 1995 onwards.

A small number of companies, e.g. Lex plc, were prepared to retain part or all of their purchased goodwill subject to annual review, that is, without regular amortisation charges. However, the most common accounting policy option was to capitalise purchased goodwill over its 'useful economic life' up to a maximum of 20 years (though two companies adopted the US option of amortising over 40 years). This was interesting because it was a concern of many respondents to the ASB's discussion paper and working paper on goodwill and intangible assets that a considerable number of companies would retain intangibles without amortisation. The supposed motivation was to avoid amortisation charges and thus increase profits. Such an expectation would, according to the working paper (ASB 1995a, p. 3), also be consistent with the hostile opposition to the capitalisation/amortisation proposals presented in the earlier exposure drafts, ED47 and ED52. Clearly it was an unfounded concern.

Table 5.5 Cumulative goodwill

	1993	1994	1995	1996	1997	1998	1999	2000
Number of companies reporting cumulative goodwill	197	198	198	189	181	169	152	132
Total number of companies	227	225	222	210	200	188	174	157
Percent of companies reporting cumulative goodwill	87	88	89	90	91	90	87	84
Cumulative goodwill written off to reserves (£bn)	72.43	78.31	96.13	101.76	113.49	105.23	94.90	82.12
Average cumulative goodwill written off per goodwill reporting company (£bn)	0.368	0.396	0.486	0.539	0.627	0.622	0.624	0.622
Total net assets (£bn)	446.8	454.6	476.8	466.1	447.3	342.0	392.6	580.5
Average total net assets per company (£bn)	1.968	2.021	2.148	2.220	2.236	1.819	2.256	3.697
Average cumulative goodwill/ average total net assets (%)	18.7	19.6	22.6	24.3	28.0	34.2	27.7	16.8

Let us consider part of the accounting policy from Lex's 2000 published accounts in respect of the balance sheet retention of goodwill without amortisation:

> Goodwill relating to the acquisition of RAC Holdings Limited has not been amortised and is subject to an annual impairment test from 2000 onwards. This is not in accordance with Schedule 4 to the Companies Act 1985 which requires that all goodwill be amortised. The directors consider that this would fail to give a true and fair view of the profit for the year and that the economic measure of performance in any period is properly made by reference only to any impairment that may have arisen. It is not practicable to quantify the effect on the grounds of this departure. Any impairment charge is included within operating profits. Goodwill attributable to other acquisitions is amortised to nil by equal annual installments over 20 years.

The appeal is to the true and fair view override, rather than the Companies Act, which is a bold step in that potentially it also overrides the FRS10 rebuttable presumption as to a 20-year life. It is unclear whether the policy decision was affected by the reported total operating loss in 2000 (an entirely pragmatic viewpoint), or by a genuine belief that the life expectancy of this particular purchased goodwill (rather than other previous purchased goodwill amounts) would have an indefinite life. Of course, there may also be some other undisclosed reason.

Despite a regulatory requirement to disclose the cumulative goodwill written off to reserves, some companies did not. Table 5.5 indicates the extent of cumulative purchased goodwill disclosure within the survey sample.

Table 5.5 has to be used with considerable caution, particularly in respect of that information which is not disclosed by companies. Firstly, a number of companies use a negative goodwill reserve as the only means of disclosing cumulative goodwill written off to reserves. One cannot be sure whether, at the time of establishing the negative goodwill reserve, all the cumulative goodwill has been recorded. For example, in 1997 Unichem plc reports a negative goodwill reserve of £208.2 million and, in the acquisition notes, cumulative goodwill written off to reserves of £360.8 million. Secondly, cumulative goodwill can be subject to restatements due to accounting policy changes following takeovers (e.g.

United News & Media plc annual report and accounts 1996), the effects of FRS7 (e.g. Simon Engineering plc annual report and accounts 1995) and for items of an undisclosed nature (e.g. Securicor plc annual report and accounts 1996).

Thirdly, the cumulative goodwill disclosures may be net balances (though I cannot be absolutely sure about this), which means they may sometimes hide the effects of negative goodwill and other adjustments, foreign exchange being a common adjustment, as well as the purchased goodwill written off to reserves. For example, and rather unusually, Brent Walker plc in 1994 and ASW Holdings in 1995 disclosed a positive goodwill reserve rather than the more typical negative goodwill reserve.

Finally, there are companies who find it is either impractical or too costly to record cumulative goodwill. For example, FKI plc in its 2000 accounts states that there is 'insufficient information' to calculate the figure in the respect of certain previous group reorganisations prior to 1989. In contrast, some companies, such as Wolseley plc, were able to capitalise all purchased goodwill previously written off to reserves—back to 1958. Many companies appear to have an arbitrary starting point, typically starting in the 1980s. The point here is that one is not strictly comparing like with like and one has to rely on year-on-year consistency in cumulative goodwill reporting (84% min to 91% max of sample size over eight years) and the overall trend in any analysis. In this latter regard, the figures are perhaps better presented as annual averages, as expressed in bottom-line percentage terms in Table 5.5.

Looking at the bottom line in Table 5.5, one can see that the year-on-year percentage increase peaks in 1998. Post FRS10, purchased goodwill is no longer to be written off to reserves, so these figures will now decline as total net assets are swelled by capitalised goodwill and the goodwill on disposals is written back, year-on-year, to the profit and loss account (the majority accounting practice). Incidentally, the large percentage drop in 2000 is because of two substantial acquisitions or mergers by Unilever plc and Vodafone plc. These two transactions increased the overall total net asset base by £140 billion. Omitting these two transactions would have yielded a goodwill to net assets ratio of approximately 22%. If one wants to see how this trend would have developed were it not for FRS10 then one needs to add back to 'cumulative purchased goodwill' and deduct from the 'total net assets' the goodwill now capitalised on the balance sheet. Also one would also need to make adjustments in respect of amortisation charges and prior year adjustments and for those companies who consistently capitalised goodwill pre FRS10. Roughly, the effect of such adjustments would be that the 1998, 1999 and 2000 average cumulative goodwill to average total net assets percentage would be restated at approximately 40%, 45% and 50%, respectively. The year-on-year restated percentage increase is not unexpected, given the substantial number of acquisitions that have occurred recently.

The significant increase in the post-FRS10 capitalisation and disclosure of purchased goodwill, if continued, means without doubt that purchased goodwill is set to become a prominent and increasingly large feature of UK balance sheets. Purchased goodwill is an 'asset', at least from a disclosure viewpoint, but to remind readers, the Accounting Standards Board acknowledges it 'is not in itself an asset' (FRS10, p. 3). The ASB states it is 'part of a larger asset, the investment, for which management remains accountable.' Indeed, management will be accountable, but for something which has an indeterminate nature and which is operationally defined by accountants as an SSAP22/FRS10 arithmetic 'difference'. Evidence from the US suggests that purchased goodwill will sometimes come to dominate the balance sheet (Jennings *et al.* 1996). This makes life difficult for financial directors, who may have to explain the use and returns from an 'asset' whose nature is described kindly by some as 'will-o'-the-wisp' (Lee 1971, 1993) and emotively by others as a 'steamy heap' (van Mesdag 1993).

BRAND ASSETS

The recognition of brands as assets, brand assets, can occur in three ways: firstly, as the result of a transaction for the outright purchase or licensing of a brand; secondly, as an extraction from the transaction for the purchase of goodwill; and thirdly, as the result of a managerial decision to include internally created brand assets on the balance sheet. In all of the reported brand accounting instances below, brand asset recognition occurred as an extraction from purchased goodwill, to be capitalised separately from it ('fair value' references in the accounting policies indicating the brand is part of an acquisition or alternatively an acquisition note linking the acquisition to a disclosed brand name). In other words, no goodwill equals no disclosure of brand assets. Table 5.6 shows movements in the number and value of sample companies recognising brand assets on their balance sheets.

In all of the instances in Table 5.6, no amortisation charge has been made to the profit and loss account and their values are subject to periodic review. The main valuation methods, where disclosed, were price premium (no companies disclosing), earnings valuation (Dalgety, United Biscuits), market value (SmithKline Beecham, Reckitt & Colman) and original/historic cost (Cadbury Schweppes, Ladbroke, Grand Metropolitan, London International Group).

In assessing the impact of FRS10 on brand asset accounting, it is important to know the reason for companies withdrawing from such disclosure in 1998, 1999 and 2000. Particularly so, if this is the start of a future trend towards the complete removal of brand assets from UK balance sheets. Of the four brand accounting withdrawals during this period, Dalgety was the result of a demerger of its group of companies. Inchcape plc was the result of a disposal of a subsidiary and with it the formerly capitalised brand. London International Group was the result of a prior year amortisation charge that effectively wrote off its brands. Whilst the introduction of FRS10 was clearly a driving force in this and other related decisions, only United Biscuits specifically cites FRS10 as the reason for a change in brand accounting policies and practices. This is examined more closely below, but first let us consider an example of some substantial acquisitions.

The £2.3 billion rise in brand asset values in 1995 (Table 5.6) was due mainly to two major acquisitions: Pet Incorporated (by Grand Metropolitan) and Dr Pepper/Seven Up (by Cadbury Schweppes). The £1.9 billion rise in brand asset values in 2000 (Table 5.6) was due to two major acquisitions: Young & Rubicam Inc. (by WPP plc) and Bestfoods/Slim-Fast (by Unilever). These acquisitions are noteworthy for the size of the acquired intangible assets relative to the purchase price (Table 5.7).

The amount of money spent on goodwill and brand assets is large by any objective standard. Indeed, it would not be an exaggeration to describe the Unilever acquisition as colossal. The capitalisation of intangible assets jumped from £0.643 billion to £26 467 billion in one year. With the first two companies in Table 5.7, brand capitalisation dominates over goodwill capitalisation, whereas the second two companies disclose most of their intangible asset value as goodwill. It is interesting that the first two are pre FRS10

Table 5.6 Brand asset disclosure on UK balance sheets

	1993	1994	1995	1996	1997	1998	1999	2000
Cadbury Schweppes plc	446	522	1 689	1 547	1 575	1 561	1 656	2 354
Grand Metropolitan plc*	2 924	2 782	3 840	3 884	–	–	–	–
Guinness plc*	1 395	1 395	1 395	1 395	–	–	–	–
Ladbroke plc (now Hilton Group plc)	377	277	277	277	277	277	277	277
London International Group	40	40	36	32	32	32	–	–
Reckitt & Colman plc (now Reckitt Benckiser)	682	1 296	1 273	1 145	1 135	1 187	1 489	1 584
United Biscuits plc	217	248	251	211	138	–	–	–
WPP plc	350	350	350	350	350	350	350	950
SmithKline Beecham plc (now GlaxoSmithKline)		776	751	688	652	644	640	632
Dalgety plc			130	130	130	–	–	–
Diageo plc (*merger)					4 995	4 727	4 875	4 875
Inchcape plc					22	19	–	–
Unilever plc								1 211
Total	6 431	7 686	9 992	9 659	9 306	8 797	9 287	11 883
Number of companies	8	9	10	10	10	8	6	7

Table 5.7 Examples of substantial company acquisitions: percentages in parentheses

	Goodwill	Brands	Total intangibles	Other assets less liabilities	Purchase price
Pet Inc. (£m)	690	1 067	1 757	17	1 774
	(39)	(60)	(99)	(1)	(100)
DPSU (£m)	564	1 132	1 696	64	1 760
	(32)	(64)	(96)	(4)	(100)
Y&R (£m)	2 819	624	3 443	−464	2 979
	(95)	(21)	116	(−16)	(100)
Bestfoods/Slim-Fast (£m)	26 651	1 166	27 817	2 744	30 561
	(87)	(4)	(91)	(9)	(100)

and the second two are post FRS10. However, the extent to which company capitalisation policies in respect of brands were affected by FRS10 is unknown. What we can say is that all four companies support to varying degrees the capitalisation of brands. Figure 5.3 gives an example of a brand accounting disclosure pre and post FRS10.

The dilemma for companies such as United Biscuits is that most other companies would have subsumed brands within goodwill. Taking a principled minority stance towards the separable recognition of brand assets, whether conceptually or pragmatically based, is fine providing others ultimately follow your lead. Otherwise, one risks turning 'principle' into 'isolation' and 'enlightenment' into perceived 'maverick behaviour'. In the absence of an increasing national trend towards separable brand asset recognition, the temptation

(a)

Balance sheet		1997	1996
Fixed assets		£m	£m
Intangible assets	Note 7	137.7	210.6
Tangible assets	Note 8	532.3	645.3
Investments	Note 10	13.5	13.3
		683.5	869.2

Accounting policy A fair value is attributed to acquired brands at the date of acquisition by the Group. They are accounted for as intangible assets. The value is calculated by multiplying the earnings of the brand by a factor determined by the brand's strength. No depreciation is provided on these assets but the directors review their value each year and the cost will be written down if, in their opinion, there has been a permanent diminution in value.

Note 7: Intangible assets	1997	1996
Brands at cost	£m	£m
At beginning of year	210.6	251.0
Exchange adjustment	(17.8)	(13.3)
Businesses disposed	(55.1)	(27.1)
At end of year	137.7	210.6

(b)

		1998	1997
Fixed assets		£m	£m
Intangible assets	Note 7	45.5	–
Tangible assets	Note 9	592.6	532.3
Investments	Note 11	10.6	13.4
		648.7	545.7

Accounting policies: intangible assets Prior year adjustment FRS10 also introduced new requirements for the recognition and measurement of intangible assets and the revenues generated by such assets in subsequent years. The Directors consider it unlikely that intangibles will be able to be distinguished from goodwill reliably enough to meet the strict requirements of FRS10. Accordingly, the value of any brands acquired in the future is likely to be subsumed within goodwill. To ensure consistency of treatment with previously acquired goodwill, all brands acquired prior to 1998 have been reclassified as goodwill and written off to reserves as a prior year adjustment.

Note 7: Intangible assets	Goodwill
	£m
Arising on acquisitions during the year	46.7
Amortisation charge for the year	(1.2)
Net book value at 2 Jan 1999	45.5

Figure 5.3   United Biscuits plc published accounts extracts

for accountants is always to return to the majority stance, particularly where the majority stance is validated, albeit to a very limited extent, by the introduction of a reporting standard such as FRS10.

With regard to United Biscuits plc (UB), its 1998 accounts show a reversal of brand accounting policies away from the separable recognition of brand assets towards their subsumption within goodwill. One of the reasons for this reversal, cited in UB's annual report, is the FRS10 requirement for 'sufficient reliability' with regard to measurement of brand assets (p. 22). However, this requirement pre-dates FRS10 and is perhaps a problem endemic to all brand assets, past and present. A better argument in favour of not recognising brands on the balance sheet is the 'lack of consistency' argument between the capitalisation of UB's post-1988 purchased brands and the decision not to capitalise pre-1988 core brands such as McVities (p. 23). There is also a valid 'lack of consistency' argument between the capitalisation of purchased brands (post 1988 or not) and the decision not to capitalise internally created brands like McVities and Penguin (pre 1988 or not).

Though speculative, it seems that the desire of UB to return to mainstream good-will/brand accounting practice is stronger than its support, conceptually, for the notion of the separable recognition of brand assets on the balance sheet. In this case, regrettably, the FRS10 'return to mainstream stance' wins over the conceptual stance towards the separable recognition of brand assets, regardless of measurement problems. UB states that the decision to remove the capitalised brands from the balance sheet has no effect on the underlying value of the business (p. 23), yet I would argue that what is not regarded as an asset can only then be regarded as an expense. The 'underlying value' is written off, at least from a disclosure viewpoint. Figure 5.3(b) shows the restated UB accounts for 1997 and 1998.

The majority stance with regard to the capitalisation of brands is that they are subsumed within purchased goodwill such that they cease to be recognised separately from it. However, there are companies, such as Aegis plc, for whom brands are of paramount importance. So that, whilst they have adopted the mainstream accounting practice of subsuming brands within goodwill on the balance sheet, they are nevertheless prepared to rebut the presumption of a 20-year life, citing the existence of brands as the justifica-tion for doing so. One may argue that it does not matter whether one calls it brands or goodwill, it still appears on the balance sheet. However, as I attempt to show in the next chapter, purchased goodwill is not an asset whereas few would doubt the 'assetness' of a brand in terms of its ability to create wealth. Consider the following accounting policy extract from Aegis's annual report and accounts for 2000:

> In the case of goodwill arising on the acquisition of Market Facts Inc., the directors are of the opinion that the goodwill has an indefinite useful economic life due to the strength of the brand, its market position, its long term profitability outlook and the Group's commitment and proven ability to enhance brand value. The financial statements depart from the specific requirements of companies legislation to amortise goodwill over a finite period in order to give a true and fair view.

COPYRIGHT

The word 'copyright' is used here as a generic term for publishing rights, titles (including newspaper titles/mastheads), music copyright, exhibition rights, and so on. A little bit of caution needs to be exercised with regard to this heading because, firstly, some companies also include databases as part of their disclosure (more properly identified under the software heading, below). Secondly, it is possible to label a newspaper title as a corporate brand (more properly identified under the brand assets heading, above). Of the six disclosing PLCs in 2000, Trinity Mirror capitalised and retained the value of its copyrights, subject to a periodic review for any diminution in value; EMI, Daily Mail and General Trust, Carlton Communications, Reed Elsevier, and United News & Media capitalised and amortised their copyright.

An example of this type of disclosure is Mirror Group plc, which was notable for the fact that in 1997 it could not determine a historic cost for its newspaper title (Figure 5.4).

Like United Biscuits, in 1998 Mirror Group reversed its policy towards the capitalisation of certain titles which it considered did not comply with FRS10. The interesting feature of this reversal is that it is related to internally created titles which were valued at £625 million (Note 11 in Figure 5.4(a)). The reversal was therefore conducted through the revaluation reserve; that is, there was no impact on profit and loss or on the related reserve.

The Mirror Group finance director readily acknowledged in the report and accounts (1998, p. 25) that the accounting adjustment did not reflect any change in the directors' opinion of the value of the group's titles but that the 'value' is not to be capitalised. One suspects that the key words here in determining whether or not these titles should be capitalised are 'readily ascertainable market value', as per FRS10. Despite having already established a value of £625 million, one suspects that doubts arose with regard to how 'readily ascertainable' that value was in relation to a market which, at best, can only be described as thin. However, from my viewpoint, this is one more example of where the requirement for 'sufficient reliability' in the measurement of intangibles dominates to the exclusion of valuations from the balance sheet. Conceptually, Mirror Group would undoubtedly acknowledge that such titles are assets and that they clearly have a value but the Mirror Group's accountants prefer to retreat to the relative security of the ASB's regulatory created reality, as per FRS10. It is a bold accountant who is prepared to risk a qualification to the accounts. Figure 5.4(b) shows revised account extracts for 1997 (restated) and 1998.

One year later Trinity had taken over the Mirror Group to form Trinity Mirror plc. It resulted in a huge increase in capitalised intangible assets, of which £1757 million related to publishing rights and titles and only £11 million related to goodwill. In the 2000 accounts, the respective figures climbed to £2005 million and £15 million. As with brand assets, the directors considered that publishing rights and titles would have an indefinite economic life and therefore would not be subject to annual amortisation. It was confirmed to me by email that the previously capitalised internally generated 'national and Scottish titles', reversed above as part of the Mirror Group's 1998 accounts, were disclosed again on the combined balance sheet of Trinity Mirror. These reversed titles were part of an acquisition for a complete business; there is now a known transaction-based amount on which to proceed with capitalisation, or more accurately recapitalisation, of those internally generated publishing rights and titles.

What a nonsense. Publishing rights are assets pre FRS10, then they are not assets post FRS10, then they are assets again on a different balance sheet. This highlights the unnecessarily restrictive application of the existing 'transactions or events' recognition

(a)

Balance sheet		1997	1996
Fixed assets		£m	£m
Intángible assets	Note 11	810	625
Tangible assets	Note 12	371	353
Investments	Note 13	18	37
		1199	1015

Note 11: Intangible fixed assets Newspaper titles £810 million (1996: £625 million). The existing titles are stated at directors' valuation which approximates to their estimate of current cost. In arriving at the estimate as at 28 December 1997, the directors have taken account of an independent professional valuation performed by Hambros Bank plc as at 2 January 1994. The valuation, which was in excess of the amount which the directors have incorporated in the financial statements, represented the sum of the amounts it was estimated could be realised if the titles together with their associated publishing rights were to be sold in market conditions as at 2 January 1994. The historic cost of these titles is not disclosed on the basis that it is not now possible to ascertain it. The newly acquired titles have been valued at £180 million as at the date of acquisition using the same valuation method as for the existing titles representing the directors' valuation of current cost and has been used as the basis for the fair value adjustment (note 26). The titles acquired in 1996 as part of the acquisition of Century Press and Publishing have similarly been valued and accordingly goodwill written off in 1996 has been credited by £0.5 m (note 21).

(b)

Balance sheet		1998	1997
Fixed assets		£m	£m
Intangible assets	Note 11	205	185
Tangible assets	Note 12	360	371
Investments in associated undertakings	Note 13	22	18
		587	574

Accounting policies The group has changed its accounting policy with regard to the accounting for the value of certain newspaper titles in order to comply with FRS10, *Goodwill and Intangible Assets*. In previous years a value of £625m was attributed to the national and Scottish titles in the balance sheet but FRS10 does not permit the value of internally generated intangible assets which do not have readily ascertainable market values to be reflected on the balance sheet. Accordingly the revaluation has been reversed as a prior year adjustment against opening shareholders' funds. This accounting adjustment does not reflect any change in the directors' opinion of the value of these titles and has no impact on the profit and loss account or on the Company's ability to pay dividends.

Note 11: Intangible assets
Movements in intangible fixed assets are as follows

	Titles	Goodwill	Total
	£m	£m	£m
Balance at 28 Dec 97 as previously reported	810	–	810
FRS10 prior year adjustment	(625)	–	(625)
Balance at 28 Dec 97 as restated for FRS10	185	–	185
Acquisitions (note 13)	14	6	20
Balance at 3 Jan 99	199	6	205

Figure 5.4 Mirror Group plc published accounts extracts

boundary within the UK definition of an asset, as discussed in the previous chapter. Specifically, the requirement for a verifiable transaction-based cost or RAMV (post FRS10) excludes valuations of certain internally generated publishing rights and titles that arise outside this context (pre FRS10), but then subsequently includes those same valuations, providing they do not exceed the known transaction-based cost of an acquisition (as where Trinity takes over the Mirror Group). Van Mesdag (1993) was right, truly 'a steamy heap'.

LICENCES AND CONCESSIONS

Here are the PLCs where licences were capitalised in 2000: pharmacy licences (Unichem, J. Sainsbury), betting office licences (Ladbroke), mineral exploration licences (Enterprise Oil), distribution rights (De La Rue), operator licences (BNFL) and telephone network licences (Vodafone).

There appear to be a wide range of accounting practices in existence. For example, at one end of the spectrum is Pearson plc, who in 2000 did not disclose any intangible assets separately from goodwill. Yet its publishing rights, television licences and brands, such as Penguin, Financial Times and Channel 5, are one of the main means of accessing its future economic benefits. At the other end of the spectrum are companies like Ladbroke (now Hilton Group), who capitalise licences based on valuations related to trading conditions and impair them accordingly. For example, page 21 of Ladbroke's 2000 annual report refers to the following information as a justification for impairment: 'Changes in Belgium legislation relating to the operation of slot machines has placed considerable doubt over the group's ability to operate these machines in the future. As a consequence of this, an impairment of £25.6 million has been recognised in respect of the licence costs and tangible fixed assets of the Belgium operation.'

Unlike United Biscuits (UB), Ladbroke retained its Hilton International brand on the balance sheet, post FRS10. And like Mirror Group's accounting treatment of its titles, Ladbroke restated its capitalised licences down to their original cost, post FRS10. Though compliant with FRS10, there is a certain inconsistency between individual intangible accounting practices in that brands are valued by 'discounting the incremental cash flows' whereas licences are 'restated at cost'. It would appear that, in contrast to UB's brand capitalisation policy, Ladbroke feels strongly enough about the public recognition and disclosure of its Hilton brand to want it on the balance sheet, regardless of the accounting requirement for 'sufficient reliability' in the measurement of its worth. There is no doubt that UB was equally serious about its brands—indeed the title of its 1998 report and accounts was 'Talking Brands'—but this did not translate into disclosure on the balance sheet. Figure 5.5 shows the published annual report and accounts extract of the Hilton Group for 2000.

PATENTS

It is typical to find the disclosure of patents as part of a general intangible heading such as 'Patents, licences and other intangibles.' Figure 5.6 is an example of its more separable disclosure.

Balance sheet		2000	1999
Fixed assets		£m	£m
Intangible assets	Note 10	1107.3	1184.9
Tangible assets	Note 11 and 12	3060.2	2857.7
Investments	Note 13	78.7	73.5
		4246.2	4116.1

Accounting policies In accordance with FRS10 and FRS11, the group capitalises acquired intangible assets (brands and betting office licences) and reviews the values annually with a view to write down if an impairment arises. Intangible assets are stated at cost less any amount written off for impairment. These are not depreciated as they are regarded as having indefinite lives.

Note 10: Intangible assets	Total	Brand name	Licences	Goodwill
	£m	£m	£m	£m
Cost at 31 Dec 1999	1223.5	276.7	200.0	746.8
Amortisation	116.2	–	18.4	97.8
NBV at 31 Dec 2000	1107.3	276.7	181.6	649.0
NBV at 31 Dec 1999	1184.9	276.7	196.6	711.6

Figure 5.5   Hilton Group plc published accounts extract

SOFTWARE AND DATABASES

Data set PLCs who in 2000 capitalised software and database assets comprised Invensys, Great Universal Stores and ICL. The annual reports of ICL refer to the capitalisation of the 'costs' of producing software, which typically refer to internal labour costs. Great Universal Stores is a little more specific in referring to the capitalisation of 'internally developed databases'. The issue of whether capitalised labour costs is a suitable proxy for the software program itself, was addressed earlier in the book. However, it is interesting to note that internally developed rather than purchased assets are now being capitalised. It is reminiscent of the Ranks Hovis McDougall case, where Ranks attempted to capitalise brands 'acquired or otherwise'. The pressure to recognise and capitalise such assets appears to be growing. For example, a call by Britannia Software to capitalise websites was rejected by the ASB (*Accountancy Age*, 1 April 1999, p. 11). Figure 5.7 shows an example of a company that capitalised software development.

DEVELOPMENT EXPENDITURE

At the initial recognition stage of an asset, the attachment of the accounting profession to transaction-based asset recognition is much stronger than it is to valuation-based

Balance sheet		1999	1998
Fixed assets		£m	£m
Intangible assets	Note 12	8.4	4.0
Tangible assets	Note 13	61.1	58.1
Investments	Note 14	3.6	2.1
		73.1	64.2

Accounting policy Intangible assets representing trademarks are recorded at cost. Trademark costs are amortised over a period of up to 10 years. Expenditure on patents is capitalised and amortised, on a unit of sale basis, over the anticipated useful life of the patent remaining when the sale of the patented product is made. Capitalised development expenditure is amortised, on a unit of sale basis, over the expected life of the product.

Figure 5.6   London International Group plc published accounts extract

Balance sheet		2000	1999
Fixed assets		£m	£m
Intangible assets	Note 14	29.0	41.4
Tangible assets	Note 15	260.8	216.2
Investments	Note 16	43.7	117.3
		333.5	374.9

Accounting policy: development expenditure The costs of producing software products are capitalised as intangible fixed assets once a detailed program design or working model has been established and commercial and financial viability has been demonstrated. These assets are amortised on a straight line basis over their estimated lives, which are usually between three and four years. Costs incurred in establishing the design or working model and the costs of maintaining existing products are written off as incurred. All other development expenditure is written off in the accounting period in which it is incurred.

Note 14: Intangible fixed assets	Software program products	Goodwill	Total
	£m	£m	£m
Cost at 31 March 2000	67.7	8.3	76.0
Accumulated depreciation	42.1	4.9	47.0
Net book value at 31 March 2000	25.6	3.4	29.0

Figure 5.7   ICL plc published accounts extract

approaches. For example, internally created intangibles may be recognised under SSAP13, *Accounting for Research and Development* (ASC 1989a), where development expenditure, under certain conditions (para 25), may be deferred to subsequent accounting periods. The expenditure is at transaction-based historic cost and the dominant accounting principle guiding its deferral is the matching principle. It is dominant in that the matching principle is applied to justify the recognition and disclosure of intangible assets, such as internally created patents, where the future economic benefits are initially capped at transaction-based cost.

This was addressed in the previous chapter under the heading of capitalised revenue expenditure. In essence, the balance sheet is used to 'park' revenue expenses to be charged through the profit and loss account over a number of years. In this regard, it shows the dominance of the matching concept over the accruals concept. As a practice it is in decline, at least from a disclosure viewpoint, down from nine companies in 1993 to four PLCs in 2000: Babcock International, Carlton Communications and Securicor and Thames Water. Figure 5.8 presents an example.

EXPLORATION EXPENDITURE

Exploration expenditure was addressed in the previous chapter under the heading of pseudo-assets. In practice, exploration costs become tangible or intangible according to operating circumstance, rather than according to their nature, and specifically whether such expenditure results in a successful mineral find or not. There is a 'conceptual versus process' approach here. The 'process' states that an asset is intangible or tangible according to operating circumstance; however, 'conceptually' it is highly unlikely that something which is intangible in nature can transmute into something which is tangible. Figure 5.9 shows an example of this intangible asset.

FINDINGS FROM THE LONGITUDINAL SURVEY

In all surveyed brand accounting companies, brand asset recognition is extracted from purchased goodwill, which arises at one moment on acquisition of a business. None of the companies surveyed disclosed the capitalisation of internally created brand assets. In the absence of an alternative accounting method, it is reasonable to surmise that there is a strong linkage between brand assets and purchased goodwill. The existing basis for the recognition of brand assets, i.e. as an extraction from purchased goodwill, is highly selective. It is hard to think of another situation where the recognition of one asset, a brand asset, is so heavily dependent on such specific one-off circumstances for the recognition of another asset, purchased goodwill. Indeed, there seems to be no logical basis to this dependency in comparison to other assets other than as an asset previously hidden among purchased goodwill.

Whether the domination of a transaction for purchased goodwill excludes other bases for recognition, particularly for internally created brand assets, is not proven conclusively but there is a strong suggestion that it does. For example, I have shown from the above brief review of the longitudinal survey that there are instances where the accounting profession is required to retreat to reliability of measurement afforded by either transaction-based cost or transaction-based RAMVs, as per FRS10. That is, disclosed intangibles that we know exist, remain within purchased goodwill (e.g. Aegis's brands); or post FRS10 they are subsumed within purchased goodwill again (e.g. UB's brands); or they are subsumed within purchased goodwill post FRS10 only to be separately capitalised again on purchase by another business (Figure 5.4).

Balance sheet		2000	1998
Intangible assets	Note 12 and 11	233.2	43.5
Tangible assets	Note 13 and 12	418.4	345.7
Investments	Note 14 and 13	114.6	37.1
		766.2	426.3

Accounting policy extract (1998) Pre-transmission *revenue* expenditure (excluding programming) in respect of the Television division is deferred and charged to the profit and loss account over the initial licence period.

Accounting policy extract (2000) Development expenditure on digital cinema is capitalised and amortisation will commence on delivery of digital systems to cinemas. All other research, development and marketing expenditure is written off as incurred, with the exception of certain programme development expenditure. ... Programme development expenditure relating to programmes which have been or anticipated to be commissioned for production is carried forward at cost.

1998 **Note 11: Intangible fixed** **assets**	Pre-transmission revenue expenditure	Publishing rights and other	Rank Film Library	Total
Group	£m	£m	£m	£m
Cost at 30 Sept 1998	30.3	2.4	30.8	63.5
Amortisation at 30 Sept 1998	17.4	1.6	1.0	20.0
Net book value at 30 Sept 1998	12.9	0.8	29.8	43.5

2000 **Note 12: Intangible fixed** **assets**	Goodwill	Publishing rights and other	Film libraries	Digital cinema development costs	Total
Group	£m	£m	£m	£m	£m
Cost at 30 Sept 2000	106.5	3.0	125.3	10.0	244.8
Amortisation at 30 Sept 2000	4.5	2.0	5.1	–	11.6
Net book value at 30 Sept 2000	102.0	1.0	120.2	10.0	233.2

Figure 5.8 Carlton Communications published accounts extracts

Whilst post FRS10 there has been some consolidation under the transaction-based umbrella of purchased goodwill, it has not been universal in application. Invensys, for example, wrote off intangible assets 'that do not meet the strict criteria for separation from goodwill under FRS10 [and therefore] have been reclassified as goodwill and written off as a prior year adjustment.' Also Invensys's capitalised intangible software development costs have now been transferred to tangible fixed assets. Such respective reclassifications and transmutations are not unique, as we saw earlier in respect of exploration costs.

Finally, cumulative goodwill previously written off to reserves is a significant figure, and as a percentage of total net assets it has been growing steadily over the pre-FRS10 period

Balance sheet		At 31 Dec 2000 $m	At 31 Dec 1999 $m
Fixed assets			
Intangible assets	Note 18	16 893	3 344
Tangible assets	Note 19	75 173	52 631
Investments	Note 20	110 753	10 109
Total fixed assets		103 819	66 084

Accounting policy extract Exploration expenditure is accounted for in accordance with the successful efforts method. Exploration and appraisal drilling expenditure is initially capitalized as an intangible fixed asset. When proved reserves of oil and gas are determined and development is sanctioned, the relevant expenditure is transferred to tangible production assets. All exploration expenditure determined as unsuccessful is charged against income. Exploration licence acquisition costs are amortised over the estimated period of exploration. Geological and geophysical exploration costs are charged against income as incurred.

Note 17: Intangible assets	Exploration expenditure $m	Goodwill $m	Other intangibles $m	Total $m
Cost 31 Dec 2000	6 106	12 055	755	18 916
Depreciation at 31 Dec 2000	690	882	451	2 023
Net book amount	5 416	11 173	304	16 893

Figure 5.9   BP Amoco plc balance sheet extract

to 1997. Though speculative, there is every indication that the problem the accounting profession had with excessive reserve depletion under SSAP22 will convert into another problem under FRS10, an increasing goodwill asset whose nature and revenue-earning potential are indeterminate. The 1998, 1999 and 2000 figures clearly show that it is set to become a prominent feature of UK balance sheets.

Part Two
Brands

6

Breaking the link between brand assets and purchased goodwill

According to FRS10,

> The goodwill arising on acquisition of a business is neither an asset like other assets
> nor an immediate loss in value. Rather, it forms the bridge between the cost of an
> investment shown as an asset in the acquirer's own financial statements and the values
> attributed to the acquired assets and liabilities in the consolidated financial statements.
> Although purchased goodwill is not in itself an asset, its inclusion amongst the assets
> of the reporting entity, rather than as a deduction from shareholders' equity, recognises
> that goodwill is part of the larger asset, the investment, for which management remains
> accountable. (ASB 1997, p. 3)

Two important features arise from the above statement. Firstly, goodwill is 'neither an asset like other assets' and therefore as a debit it can only be an expense. However, it is not an expense because there is no 'immediate loss in value' to warrant its write-off to profit, past or present. As 'purchased goodwill is not in itself an asset' and also not an expense, it begs the question, What type of debit is it? It is 'part of the larger asset [larger than what?], the investment, for which management remains accountable', but investments are typically regarded as assets. One could reasonably conclude that this tortuous exercise is leading nowhere except for one inescapable fact—purchased goodwill is to be disclosed on the balance sheet and therefore it is an asset if only in presentational terms. In contrast, for example, the Australian position (AASB 1996) is that 'goodwill comprises the future economic benefits from unidentifiable assets which, because of their nature, are not normally individually recognised' (AASB1013, para 5.1.1). Initially, there is no suggestion that any part of goodwill may simply be an overpayment and therefore an expense. Indeed, the AASB emphasises the conceptual point that there is no difference between an internally generated goodwill asset and a purchased goodwill asset other than in respect of reliability of measurement (para 5.1.2).

The second feature of the opening paragraph arises from the reference to goodwill as a 'bridge between the cost of an investment shown as an asset in the acquirer's own financial statements and the values attributed to the acquired assets and liabilities in the consolidated financial statements.' The two key words here are 'cost' and 'value' or, specifically, between the transaction-based *cost* of acquiring a business and the value, so-called *fair value*, of the identified assets acquired. In effect, one has a mismatch between two different measurement methods, cost and fair values, which is confirmed by the definition of purchased goodwill itself as a measured 'difference' (FRS10, 1997, p. 9), rather than in any attempt to address its constituent nature. Specifically, 'the difference between the *cost* of an acquired entity and the aggregate of the *fair values* of that entity's identifiable assets and liabilities' (emphasis added). In other words, purchased goodwill exists, at least in part, from the inability of the accounting profession to agree on a single measurement method with which to account. Indeed, adherence to multiple measurement methods was accepted in the UK Statement of Principles (ASB 1999).

Highlighted here are some regulatory examples of the use of multiple measurement methods in the disclosure of purchased goodwill. Purchased goodwill can be variously and often loosely defined.

Canadian Institute of Chartered Accountants

The Canadian Institute of Chartered Accountants (CICA 1974, section 1580.54) defines it as 'the difference between cost and the acquiring company's interest in the identifiable net assets.' There is no mention of fair values, just 'cost'.

United States Financial Accounting Standards Board

The US Financial Accounting Standards Board (FASB 1970a, APB16, para 87) says, 'the excess of the cost of the acquired company over the sum of the amounts assigned to identifiable assets acquired less liabilities assumed should be recorded as goodwill.' Again, there is no mention of fair values even though the use of such values is commonplace. In this context 'cost' is also broadly defined. For example, where assets are purchased other than for cash, 'cost', according to FASB (1970a), is either the fair value of the consideration given or the fair value of the property acquired, whichever is clearly more evident. Equally, where an asset is acquired by incurring liabilities, 'cost' is the present value of the amounts to be paid (APB16, para 67). Likewise, with regard to FAS141 on business combinations (FASB 2001, para 20), 'a *cash* payment by an acquiring entity shall be used to measure the *cost* of an acquired entity. Similarly, the *fair values* of other assets distributed as consideration, such as marketable securities or properties, and the fair values of liabilities by an acquiring entity shall be used to measure the *cost* of an acquired entity' (emphasis added).

International Accounting Standards Committee

The International Accounting Standards Committee (IASC 1998, IAS22, para 41) states that 'any excess of the cost of the acquisition over the acquirer's interest in the fair value of the identifiable assets and liabilities acquired as at the date of the exchange transaction should be described as goodwill and recognised as an asset.' Cost is defined as 'the amount of cash or cash equivalents paid or the fair value, at the date of the exchange, of the other purchase consideration given by the acquirer in exchange for control over the net assets of the enterprise' (*ibid.*, para 21). We see again the use of multiple measurement bases.

Australian Accounting Standards Board

The Australian Accounting Standards Board (AASB 1996, AASB1013, para 5.7) specifies that 'goodwill which is purchased by the entity must be measured as the excess of the cost of acquisition incurred by the entity over the fair value of the identifiable net assets acquired.' Firstly, as referred to previously, the AASB has identified goodwill as an unidentifiable *asset* (para 5.1.1) from which only the purchased goodwill is to be recognised by the entity (para 5.1.2). It therefore excludes internally generated goodwill. Secondly, the identified goodwill is then measured, as above (para 5.7). This is a logical sequence of events. With the other regulatory bodies, the measurement determines the basis for recognition as an asset, as an expense, or in the case of ASB, as 'the invest-ment'. However, the AASB subsequently undermines some of this logic by stating that to the extent that the cost of acquisition incurred by the entity exceeds the fair value of the identifiable net assets *but the difference does not constitute goodwill*, such difference must be recognised immediately as an expense in the profit and loss account (para 5.8). In paragraph 5.7 they proclaim the asset status of goodwill and in paragraph 5.8 they leave themselves the option that some of it may actually be an expense. Of course, this begs the question as to what proportion of the goodwill 'difference' is unidentifiable assets or an expense. It also alludes to the problematic constituent nature of goodwill itself. Finally, as with the other regulatory bodies, the 'cost of acquisition' is interpreted in different ways, including fair values where non-monetary assets are exchanged. However, it has to be said that the AASB, wherever possible, has sensibly used the term 'purchase consideration' instead of 'cost' so as not to confuse 'cost' with 'value'.

New Zealand Accounting Standards Review Board

The New Zealand Accounting Standards Review Board (ASRB 1990, SSAP8, para 4.57) says that 'under the purchase or equity methods, where the fair values ascribed to net identifiable assets exceed the cost of the investment the balance will represent a discount on acquisition. Where the cost exceeds the fair value of the net assets the balance will represent a premium (goodwill).' Here again 'cost' is capable of multiple measurements, including fair values where securities are involved (para 4.27).

Shortcomings of these definitions

None of the above definitions of goodwill addresses the nature of goodwill as an asset, other than as an operating definition. They are universally focused on measurement methods; take one figure from another and abracadabra the difference is goodwill. Baxter (ASB 1995c, p. 16) refers to this difference as 'the accountant's self-inflicted headache'. He cites the example of a pair of china shepherd figures each costing £100, which as a pair are valued at £1000. The £800 difference between the two measurement bases, which Baxter chooses to characterise in terms of 'assets versus cash flows' (p. 17), rather than 'transaction cost versus valuations', is called goodwill. He suggests:

> A gap between the two answers is not unlikely, and does not prove the existence of some latent extra thing. The 'whole' and the 'parts' are here different economic units. ... If we split off some of the value to represent independent assets, then what is left is not one more such asset but the remainder of the stream. This certainly is valuable; but it is not a detachable thing like other assets. It is instead a fraction of the subsidiary; its value and life depend on the subsidiary's value and life. Whenever the accountant splits up a market unit into artificial bits ('allocation') he is asking for trouble.

The point to note from Baxter's explanation is that it is measurement based. The £800 difference is presented in terms that the whole (£1000) is greater than the disclosed parts (£100 × 2). However, there is nothing to prevent the accountant from disclosing the asset as a pair with a fair value of £1000 if he or she chooses to do so. The decision to be made is whether one discloses the *cost* (£100 × 2) or the *valuation* (£1000). The mismatch of measurement bases is a valid point in the context of a business acquisition but the comparison to the purchase of china figures is perhaps a poor example. The total *value* of the assets (£1000) is normally lower, not greater, than the *cost* of acquisition (£100 × 2), the difference (£800) being goodwill, or as Baxter puts it, a 'consolidation difference' in the context of a business acquisition. The use of china figures as an example implies that the difference arises from synergistic gains, which is not necessarily the case. It could, more pertinently, be said to arise from a mismatch of measurement methods alone. Certainly, that is what the above goodwill definitions appear to show—mixed measurements.

The important point is that the difference caused by the mixing of acquisition *cost* less the *value* of acquired assets is limited or capped by the transaction-based cost of acquiring a business. The reporting of transactions or events clearly dominates in the recognition process (ASB 1999, para B4.1). All that remains is to decide how to order this process by specifying and defining the classes of items or elements such as assets and expenses (para B4.2). Thus, goodwill can switch from expense element to asset element within a transaction- or event-based view of business at the regulation of accountants. There is no apparent need to address whether by nature an item is an asset or not, because no such recognition criteria currently exist. I seek to remedy that situation.

ASB (1999, para B4.2) tentatively suggests that recognition criteria could be used to avoid identifying the elements within financial statements. I would argue that they could be used to complement those elements, thus making recognition a more robust process, enabling one, for example, to distinguish more clearly the difference between assets and expenses. The ASB suggests that the use of such criteria is not viable because no recognition criteria have been developed which provide clear and comprehensive answers to the questions posed during the recognition process without introducing circularity by, for example, referring to generally accepted accounting principles. I disagree. I introduce some asset recognition criteria taken from the legal literature and I apply them to goodwill, to see whether goodwill passes the test as an identifiable asset. I am not saying the criteria are comprehensive or robust but they represent a good start down the road towards asset recognition according to its nature rather than, at present, on its ability to produce wealth. It is also an approach which is unfettered by a transaction- or event-based view of business reality, such that many intangibles could qualify as assets.

The title of this chapter implies that there is link between the disclosure of purchased goodwill and brand assets. I intend to show using these recognition criteria that goodwill is not an asset and therefore any linkage of another asset to it is conceptually unfounded. But first I need to show how that linkage operates.

BRAND ACCOUNTING WITHIN THE CONTEXT OF GOODWILL ACCOUNTING

One suspects that from a marketing perspective the above subtitle should be reversed since goodwill (customer loyalty, business reputation, etc.) is probably regarded by marketers as a by-product of a successful brand. From an accounting perspective the subtitle is correctly stated, since according to Exposure Draft 52 (ED52):

> The term brand is used to describe what is generally regarded for accounting purposes as goodwill: that is, a combination of factors which is expected to produce enhanced earnings in the future. . . . This interpretation is confirmed by the fact that the most

commonly used methods of evaluating both goodwill and brands involve the use of multiples or present values of projected future earnings. It has therefore been concluded that for accounting purposes brands are subsumed within goodwill and should be accounted for accordingly. (ASC 1990, p. 10)

However, from the evidence presented in the longitudinal survey, it was clear that a few notable PLCs, such as Diageo, Cadbury Schweppes and Reckitt Benckiser, were clearly ignoring the advice given in ED52 through the inclusion of brands as assets on their respective balance sheets. Indeed, some support for the separate recognition of brand assets is given by Hodgson *et al.* (1993, p. 149), who state:

Occasionally it is possible to be quite definite, as, for example in the case of accounting for brands—in our theory these are identifiable intangible activities and not what we have defined here to be goodwill. This is directly in disagreement with the opinion expressed in ED52 (ASC 1990). However such clear cut instances are likely to be unusual.

In general, though not in the unusual case of Ranks Hovis McDougall plc (Hart and Murphy 1998, p. 98), brands may, for accounting purposes, be extracted from the goodwill on acquisition of a business (Table 6.1).

I will make repeated reference to the lettered columns in Table 6.1 over the next few pages. Column B shows the post-acquisition position of the company with goodwill being regarded as an asset (usually depreciated). If one regards goodwill, in common with tangible assets, as a source of future revenue-earning potential, then one may subscribe to this view of the balance sheet. However, if goodwill is regarded as too fickle in nature and offering little certainty as to the amount and duration of future revenues, then one may seek to write it off as quickly as possible, usually to reserves, as shown in column C. Whilst both methods were acceptable from an accounting viewpoint, column C was the dominant allowable method under the UK Statement of Standard Accounting Practice 22 (ASC 1989b, p. 8). However, effective from 23 December 1998 (ASB 1997), the UK accounting profession has altered its position with regards to goodwill (FRS10) to make column B the only allowable method for the recognition of purchased goodwill. This brings the UK 'into line' with the US and dominant European accounting practices. So something that was not generally regarded as an asset at least for the past decade now suddenly becomes an asset and recognisable as such on the balance sheet.

Table 6.1 The accounting disclosure of brands

	A Pre acquisition	B Goodwill asset	C Goodwill and brand write-off	D Brand asset	E Goodwill and brand asset
Assets					
Cash (£m)	500	400	400	400	400
Other assets (£m)	500	560	560	560	560
Goodwill (£m)		40		20	20
Brands (£m)					20
Financed by					
Capital (£m)	800	800	800	800	800
Reserves (£m)	200	200	160	180	200

Essentially, the goodwill accounting debate focused on whether to write it off immediately (column C), to write it off gradually (column B plus annual depreciation) or not to write it off but to retain it as a long-term asset on the balance sheet (column B). It was a long-standing debate (Dicksee 1897) with, until recently, no proper resolution to it in terms of a single policy or practice. In the meantime, accountants became increasingly aware of the size of goodwill and the effect that its write-off was having on balance sheet reserves. For example, the EMI Group annual report 2000 showed negative reserves and negative net equity mainly as a result of adopting the column C preferred accounting practice. In other words, on paper they were insolvent, whereas in reality the opposite was correct. Historically, a way of minimising reserve depletion was to extract from the goodwill write-off an amount which related to brand assets and to show this as a separate asset on the balance sheet (column D). In respect of column D, the net effect of extracting brands (£20 million) from the goodwill (£40 million) normally written off to reserves (£200 million − £40 million = £160 million) and showing them as brand assets on the balance sheet instead, was that assets and reserves increased by £20 million, thus improving the asset base and gearing but reducing performance measures such as return on capital employed.

Note that the brand asset values in column D only existed within the context of purchased goodwill. The £40 million goodwill figure therefore represented an upper and perhaps sometimes unrealistic limit to any brand asset valuation extracted from it. Also the value of the extracted brand asset was reflected on the balance sheet at the time of acquisition only; it might have appreciated a over time. An appreciation in the value of a brand asset would not currently be shown in the accounts on the grounds of prudent practice, unlike revaluations of other tangible fixed assets such as land and buildings, for example, Queens Moat Properties plc hotels (1997 report and accounts). In addition, because the column D practice did not recognise brand assets arising independently of purchased goodwill, a situation could arise where some purchased brands were included on the balance sheet and non-purchased, internally created brands were excluded from it. To repeat, Grand Metropolitan plc (now part of Diageo plc) included the purchased Burger King brand on the balance sheet but excluded the home-grown or internally created Croft brand (Croft Original sherry).

In the absence of a specific brand accounting standard, the situation remained confused with no clear evidence emerging as to whether the decision to account for brands was being made by companies because they fully embraced the brand asset concept, or whether it was based entirely on pragmatic considerations such as avoiding excessive reserve depletion. Such considerations were typically restricted to the boardroom. Avoiding excessive reserve depletion, for example, improves gearing/leverage and can sometimes assist a board in surmounting stock exchange rules on maximum levels of gearing/leverage when raising additional capital funds without recourse to shareholders (stockholders).

Given that brand accounting vis-à-vis goodwill accounting is a relatively recent phenomenon and that brand accounting is derived from goodwill accounting, then one suspects that the decision to account for brand assets has been greatly influenced by pragmatic considerations. If true, the accountancy profession has cast aside any justification for the inclusion of brands on the balance sheet based on some form of conceptual reasoning, in favour of 'window dressing' the accounts. Effectively the current debate over goodwill and brand accounting methods (columns A to E) has shifted the focus of academic attention to what Murphy (1990a) described as something of a technical accounting sideshow.

For example, no attempt is made to create a basis for recognition and disclosure of a brand asset independently of any goodwill figure. Hence, according to Kennedy (1998, p. 8), the ASB is unlikely to be concerned about whether brand assets are separately disclosed from purchased goodwill because they both, post FRS10, now appear as assets on the balance sheet (column E), thus having no material effect on reported profits or net assets (contrast columns B and E in Table 6.1).

As the subtitle suggests, brand accounting occurs within the context of purchased goodwill accounting, but if a brand is an asset, it should be recognisable in its own right, independently of purchased goodwill. Indeed, I will break that linkage in the next section of this chapter. Also if, by definition, brands are assets, their existence should not necessarily be dependent on the existing asset definition requirement for them to be the result of a 'transaction' or purchase, because there are many highly successful internally generated or non-purchased brand assets in existence, such as Coca-Cola and Microsoft. I will address the issue of brand asset definition in the next chapter.

I will now show that whilst brands can be regarded as assets, purchased goodwill is not, by nature, an asset. Purchased goodwill should therefore be written off whilst brand assets should be capitalised, leading to an overall increase in the disclosed asset base where this relates to internally created intangible assets.

SEPARATING BRAND ASSETS FROM PURCHASED GOODWILL

To assess whether purchased goodwill is by nature an asset, there needs to be some form of a benchmark by which to judge its characteristics in relation to other assets and, in particular, intangible assets such as brand assets. This is set out in the following descriptive framework. Much of it is based on an adaptation of work first presented by Honoré (1961). None of the eleven characteristics of an asset, discussed below, is a necessary constituent of an asset, since reporting entities can be recognised to own something in a restricted sense where one or more of the characteristics are not met. However, the greater the number of characteristics that are applicable to an item, the more thoroughly one can regard a reporting entity's asset as recognisable in its financial statements. Some of these characteristics have also been picked by other authors such as Pallot (1990), who regards ownership of assets as a bundle of rights: to manage, for benefits, to sell or destroy, etc.

The right to control

The exclusive, physical (or constructive) control of property is a fundamental criterion for the recognition of an asset. Within the accounting domain, the right to exercise control is the result of past transactions or events. However, the recognition of past transactions or events is hardly sufficient; it must be for the purposes of appropriation. Hence it is possible for a firm to control an asset for the purposes of appropriation when that asset does not necessarily arise from recognisable transactions or events, such as internally generated brand assets. Appropriation, that is taking and using an item for one's own use, requires one to be in possession of the asset and, in the vast majority of cases, it is secured by ownership or by legal rights of access.

Any legal system must accord the right to be put in control of something valuable. It must also assure that such control cannot be terminated arbitrarily or appropriated by others without permission, which can easily occur when possession is not legally determined; for example, the duplication of an internally generated brand that has not been trademark registered. In the absence of such formalities there is no physical artefact, and preventing its appropriation by would-be copiers of it becomes more problematic. In contrast, where a brand is trademarked it takes on a legally separable identity, the accompanying artefact being the registration document. In the absence of control, there is no asset. And in the absence of legal ownership or legal rights of access to assets, it is impossible to have a functioning entity.

With regard to the control of purchased goodwill, much depends on its constituent nature. For example, if one speculates that the purchased goodwill comprises intangible attributes such as business custom and reputation, then its appropriating capabilities appear to be inextricably linked to the control of the other assets of a business. In contrast, if one speculates that purchased goodwill simply arises from a mismatch of measurement bases, or that it represents an overpayment, then there is no power to appropriate and therefore there is nothing to control. One of the problems associated with purchased goodwill is as a measured 'difference'; the right to control it (whatever 'it' is) requires its nature to be recognised.

The right to use

The term 'use' can have a broad or narrow interpretation, with the notion here pertaining to the business entity's use and enjoyment of the asset, including its use in creating wealth. The fact that certain uses are restricted does not diminish the content of ownership and/or legal rights of access, though it may reduce the range of choice open to the owner. Remember the worked-out opencast coal mine example in Part One.

With regard to purchased goodwill, the right to use it is not conditional on it being recognisable in terms of its nature and/or as a resource. Nor is it necessary to recognise it as a separable asset in order to use it. If, for example, goodwill comprises as yet unidentifiable wealth-creating assets, such as brand assets, then these can be used in addition to the other wealth-creating assets of a business.

The right to manage

Contracting with others over the wealth derived from the use of an asset is the essence of management. Specifically, this includes the right to admit others to one's property, the power to permit others to use one's things, and to set limits to such permission. It can even involve contracting over the deliberate redundancy of an asset where there is economic advantage to one party in doing so. Part of the questionnaire in Chapter 3 was directed to that effect.

The right to manage goodwill, that is the right to admit or permit others to use goodwill and also, to set limits to its use, presupposes that managers can recognise its nature and control it (see above). So if goodwill comprises business reputation, who in their right mind would wish to buy it separately from the business as a whole? Whilst acknowledging that contracting with others over the use of assets is the essence of management, it seems highly unlikely that anyone would wish to do so with regard to goodwill alone. It may well be that purchased goodwill is hiding previously unrecognised assets such as brand assets. However, any contracting arrangements would be likely specifically to recognise brands either individually or generally as part of an overall business acquisition; for example, the right to use the Rolls-Royce name by BMW. If managers were to attempt to contract for goodwill alone, they would probably need to define something that so far has defied definition other than in terms of a 'difference'.

The right to income

The right to income has always loomed rather significantly in any discussion of the rights of ownership or access, especially in respect of the difference between income and capital resources. For example, in respect of the US and UK asset definitions, the importance of future economic benefits is perhaps overemphasised to the point where the recognition of a capital resource is excluded from the definitions. The *effect* is to give prominence to income without any assurance as to the *cause* or resource used to create such economic benefits. Pallot (1990) in a response to Mautz (1988) argues that 'the term "asset" carries with it connotations that are broader than just the direction of cash flows.' Assets have a resource dimension (where a resource is that which produces benefits) and a property dimension (where property is taken to be legally sanctioned rights over things and between persons with respect to things). Thus it is possible for a business to enjoy a property dimension and a latent resource dimension, as with land that is unused but which nevertheless retains unexplored mineral deposits. There is a right to income, but just because that income remains unrealised does not mean it ceases to be an asset. Also one needs to be careful about where that income could be coming from. Capitalised exploration cost, for example, is an inappropriate substitute for capitalised mineral deposits since the mineral deposits rather than the exploration cost represent the true capital source of the subsequent incomes.

The right to income from goodwill is linked to the income from the other assets of a business and is typically associated with the income from extra sales volumes and price premiums arising from fickle attributes such as business reputation or established custom. Identifying the income from such attributes is highly problematic but the ASB attempts it in terms of income-generating units (IGUs), where the total income generated by a business is broken down into manageable units (ASB 1998). Specifically, where a group of assets, liabilities and associated goodwill is identified as generating income that is largely independent of the reporting entity's other income streams (FRS11, p. 6). The accountant gazes into his or her crystal ball to determine from the assets within a group, the present value of the future cash flows from their continued use or their net realisable values, whichever is higher. This is then compared to the existing carrying values of the assets of that group to determine whether any impairment in value has taken place. The point here is not to digress into impairment reviews but to highlight in the next paragraph the accounting profession's approach towards the income generated by goodwill and intangibles within an IGU.

The first point to note is that the present value of cash flow incomes can determine asset values. This is consistent with the definition of an asset as something which produces future economic benefits and also with a viewpoint of assets that is entirely measurement based. However, there is also a degree of circularity here in that what an asset produces, in terms of cash flow income, determines what an asset is, rather than what an asset is and how it is used determining what an asset produces. It is an economic view of income, which differs from the accounting view of income. Economic cash flow incomes are future based whereas accounting incomes (mainly sales incomes) are historic and current. One is crystal ball gazing, the other is current fact. Accounting incomes also differ from economic cash flow incomes in that they reflect the effect of accounting concepts such as accruals. So when one talks about the 'right to income', an important prerequisite is which income, economic or accounting?

Finally, determining the cash flow income for the IGU obviously avoids determining the income from problematic component elements, such as goodwill, other than in terms of arbitrary allocations within the IGU. And let us look at these allocations, for example, where the IGU is deemed to be impaired. Any impairment other than in respect of specific assets is first allocated to goodwill, then to capitalised intangibles and finally to tangible assets (ASB 1998, para 48). It reflects a mindset that is still stuck in the nineteenth century. Thus, in general terms, if the assets of Coca-Cola were to be impaired then the brand name, either as part of goodwill or separately from it, would be one of the first assets to be written off whilst the bottling plants would remain. Personally, given the choice between the right to income from the brand name or the right to income from the bottling plants, I know which one I would choose. The brand name is everything: who wants to buy John Doe cola instead of Coke? I know accountants think they are being prudent by retreating to the security of tangible assets but it is actually imprudent where the real income creators for many companies are tied up in intangible assets. Indeed, it is even more imprudent when one considers that the brand name may not appear on the balance sheet anyway, regardless of any impairment review. Similarly, for example, it is totally nonsensical for pharmaceutical companies to disclose tangible assets on the balance sheet while not disclosing the mainstays of their business—their internally generated pharmaceutical drug patents and brands.

If the right to income from these intangible assets is present in the accounts then it seems logical that the right to the capital tied up in them should also be disclosed. The important point is whether that should be separate from goodwill.

The right to capital

This right comprehends the power to alienate an asset, or to consume it, or to destroy or waste it. Remember the earlier example of the oil-rich owners of a patent for a safe, cheap, compact and highly efficient source of generating electricity who may, in their own interest, simply not use it. Thus it may exist as legal property, it may have the potential to produce great wealth and yet in practice never do so. This represents an important departure from the existing definitions of an asset in that, firstly, assets do not necessarily have to produce income, though this is a desirable characteristic (see the right to income). Secondly, the action of alienating, consuming or destroying specific assets assumes that they have separable identities from the other assets of a business.

With regard to purchased goodwill, it is possible to argue that it is not the main focus or product of a transaction; it is actually a by-product of a transaction. No one sets out to purchase the capital associated with a 'difference' (purchased goodwill) for its own sake. It simply arises because the purchaser of the identifiable, separable assets of a business is prepared to pay a premium collectively to obtain them. It may well be that the purchasers are paying the premium for previously unidentified assets, such as brand assets, in which case they can be separately recognised. Conversely, it may well be that the purchasers are willing to sacrifice some of the future earning potential of the other separable assets through the payment of a premium simply for the right to the capital of these assets.

Once one has decided which of the two stances is appropriate then this, to a large extent, should dictate the choice of accounting method—to capitalise or to write off. It seems to be a case of 'putting the cart before the horse' to have endless debates about the choice of goodwill accounting method when, in the first place, its capital status as an asset is somewhat dubious.

The right to security

The issue here is the owner's expectation that ownership and/or legal rights, unless legally determined otherwise, shall run in perpetuity assuming solvency and behaviour consistent with accepted social norms. With regard to purchased goodwill, given its indeterminate nature, it seems unlikely that goodwill offers any security. No right-minded banker would accept goodwill, on its own, as security or settlement for a loan.

Transmissibility

Transmissibility assumes the existence of an artefact so that the person inheriting it can say that they have obtained it and now control it, even if the artefact is simply a document saying one is the proud beneficiary of a right to a trademarked brand or registered patent. No one can enjoy something after death, but an interest in an asset that is transmissible to a successor is clearly more valuable than one that stops at death. To the extent that transmissibility is restricted then one's property is diminished. Now, where is the artefact in respect of purchased goodwill? There is no such artefact. Obviously, there is a documented contract for the purchase of a business but it is by no means certain that goodwill will be mentioned in it. More typically, it is a by-product, as referred to above.

The right to the transmissibility of goodwill alone assumes that it is separable from the other assets of a business. Indeed, it is a test of an asset's separable nature that it can be transferred and be capable of being used, whether upon death or otherwise, independently of the other assets of a business. For example, it could be argued that a central heating boiler is part of a larger asset, a house, yet they both possess a characteristic which seems to be absent from goodwill, namely they can be separated, be transferred and used independently of each other. Insofar as goodwill has any capital, the transmissibility of it is inextricably linked to the other assets of a business.

The absence of a term

Along with security, this characteristic comprises the owner's interest in something that can be referred to as 'duration'. Different legal systems convey different interests over time. The interests of the owner are best served by a determinable time horizon where longer is more valuable than shorter. The absence of a term means that full ownership runs in perpetuity.

The absence of a term for goodwill means that potentially it has a 'life' which exists in perpetuity. Much academic energy has been expended in debating the length of that 'life', which has generally ranged from zero to an indefinite life. The reality is that, given its indeterminate nature, no one really knows how long it will exist, assuming it exists other than as a 'difference'. If, for example, it comprises attributes such as business reputation then this can be quickly destroyed through careless or reckless acts, for example, the former Ratners plc chairman Gerald Ratner publicly referring to his 'crap' products.

In contrast, there are surveys which show that brands can be long-lived, such as those conducted periodically by Interbrand plc. Certainly, where a brand is trademarked the duration can be indefinite, providing the owner renews the registration every ten years. Also, providing the 'right to use' is *actually* exercised, otherwise after five years the validity of the registration can be challenged.

The prohibition of harmful use

Ownership or access to an asset does not include the right to harm others. An asset is more than a set of institutional arrangements defining who may use, control or benefit from an asset. An asset is also the legal ability to impose costs on others. In addition, since the rights structure of modern assets indicates who must pay to have their interests protected against the costs imposed by another party, improper use of an asset is often prohibited. For example, the right of car manufacturers to pollute the atmosphere is partly passed on to the customer in terms of the increased expense of catalytic converters and stringent gas emissions tests.

With regard to purchased goodwill it is hard to see how something which is defined as a 'difference' can do any harm. With regard to brands it is not possible to trademark register an immoral mark but that would not prevent branding, and thus a degree of harm, outside these legal boundaries. How successful an offensive brand would be is unknown. Whether one, for example, would regard the brand FCUK as offensive is simply a question of personal perception and clever marketing. However, it would seem reasonable to assume, in general, that an offensive brand would not be successful other than where it was in response to a short-term fad. Harmfulness in this context is a relative concept and a changing concept as tastes and perceptions change; a sexually titillating picture may be pleasing to some and offensive to others. It is also relative in a macroeconomic context. For example, the exclusive legal rights to an intangible asset can provide economic advantage at the microeconomic level, but if too successful, they can fall foul of antitrust legislation where the competitive advantage appears to be monopolistic.

Liability to execution

Full ownership involves the liability of the owner's interest to be used to settle debts. In the absence of such provisions, property would become a vehicle for defrauding creditors, and national income would suffer accordingly as those with liquid capital would be wary of lending it to those with assets lacking this proviso. Certain intangible assets have the potential, particularly where they are underpinned by legal recognition (such as a trademarked brand asset), to be sold to provide the means for the settlement of liabilities. However, the same cannot be said of purchased goodwill independently of the other assets of a business; see the right to security. No one in their right mind would purchase goodwill for its own sake.

The right to residuary character

This characteristic refers to a situation where the ownership rights to the capital lapse, perhaps through the expiration of a trademark. There must be social rules for deciding what to do, for whatever reason, where the pre-existing ownership rights to an asset are no longer present. For example, a registered trademark requires renewal every ten years.

1. The existence and value of purchased goodwill are entirely dependent on the circumstances of a transaction for the purchase of a business rather than being based on a recognition of its nature and/or resource. These circumstances mean that recognition is based on a definitional or rule-driven measurement exercise which, unusually, is capable of producing a negative as well as a positive goodwill asset. No other 'asset' can appear on either side of the balance sheet simply because of the way it has been measured.
2. The rule-driven measurement of purchased goodwill is only valid for one point in time, that is, at the date of the acquisition of a business. Thereafter, the amount of goodwill will vary according to operating and economic circumstance, strategic decisions and other unknown variables; that is, it will become 'so susceptible to variation as to have no enduring quality, such as durable assets, nor any exchange value to a going concern' (Chambers 1966).
3. As a 'difference' arising from a transaction, purchased goodwill is inseparable from the other assets acquired as part of a purchase for a business and, as a result:

   (a) unlike most assets, no one in their right mind would purchase goodwill separately from the other assets of a business
   (b) unlike most assets, purchased goodwill is highly unlikely to be used to settle debts or used as collateral to raise loans

4. It arises from an operating rather than a constitutive definition, which simply tells one what to do, not what constitutes its nature or why it should be accounted in a particular way.

Figure 6.1   Attributes of purchased goodwill

In accounting terms, purchased goodwill has no residuary character in that the ownership rights to its capital, insofar as they exist, lapse once it is fully amortised or written off. Another argument exists: purchased goodwill only exists in accounting terms, not in reality, and any residuary characteristic has nothing to do with the lapse of capital but simply with what is left over from a measurement exercise. In other words, it is a residual figure right from the start of its accountancy-created existence. Accountants equally have the means not to create it, such as when they adopt the UK merger method or the former US pooling of interests method of accounting for business combinations. Under these circumstances, when similar-sized companies merge through the exchange of shares, the accounts of the two companies combine without the need for goodwill. The point here is not whether a merger method of accounting is any better than an acquisition/purchase method, which creates goodwill, it is simply that the rules which accountants choose to apply or not to apply to purchased goodwill, under differing business circumstances, can give rise to a residual figure and problematic asset (?) which is of their own (rule) making.

Summary

Purchased goodwill is not an asset. This conclusion is reached by assessing purchased goodwill against the benchmark established by the above descriptive framework. In support of this conclusion the main characteristic weaknesses of a so-called purchased goodwill asset can summarised in Figure 6.1.

It follows that if goodwill is not an asset then there is no need for brand assets to be subsumed within a dubious purchased goodwill asset heading on the balance sheet.

Brand asset recognition then becomes what it should always have been, a process of separable recognition unattached to goodwill. If you remember, support for the separable recognition of brand assets on the balance sheet was given by Hodgson *et al.* (1993). They state that 'the problem of accounting for intangibles is partly one of measurement and partly one of disclosure.' However, I have argued in Chapter 1 for a more fundamental approach based on the simple premise that one should first define and recognise the nature and/or resource of a purchased goodwill asset before consideration is given to its measurement and disclosure. Whilst purchased goodwill is operationally defined, the descriptive framework shows that it does not possess many asset-related characteristics. It may well conform to the existing definitions of an asset, but until one can be more specific about its nature and/or resource, no one is too sure exactly what it is.

There are those who argue that goodwill hides assets, such as brand assets, which can often be rescued from the never-never land of goodwill (Vaughan 1972). Never-never land is imaginary and my preference is not to rescue anything from it, especially something as potentially valuable as brand assets. That said, as was shown in the longitudinal survey, there are a few notable companies who extract from purchased goodwill a number of brand assets and then disclose them separately on their balance sheets. For most other companies, brand assets are subsumed within purchased goodwill and, it can be argued, that as purchased goodwill is now capitalised, the brands subsumed within it are also being capitalised, albeit not as a separate disclosure. Obviously I believe that both internally generated brand assets and purchased brand assets should be separately disclosed on the balance sheet, and that the attachment to goodwill is a false one, as demonstrated in this chapter. What is actually driving this attachment is that the goodwill 'difference' is transaction based and that the requirement for past transactions or events is the dominant characteristic. I showed the strengths and weaknesses of this asset recognition boundary in Part One. I also suggested an alternative asset recognition boundary based on recognition of an artefact with a legally separable identity. I will develop that further in relation to brand assets in the next chapter.

7

The definition and accounting recognition of brand assets

A television transmitter and receiving television set are part of a process that simply encodes, transmits and then decodes a two-dimensional view of reality. The transmission process is an example of a 'hard' system where the boundaries to its existence and operation are well defined and delineated. Contrast this process with a 'soft' system, such as the accounting rules for the recognition of an intangible asset, where its boundaries are difficult to define, especially in respect of the disclosure of internally generated ones. In a soft systems approach, human beings attribute meaning to the reality they perceive using intellectual skills such as inductive and deductive reasoning. Humans are constantly negotiating with each other over interpretations of the world and it is through this process that they are able to develop rules for coping with it. With such an approach, commonality of purpose becomes important as a means of obtaining acceptance and authority for one view of the world. Hence, in respect of the definition of an asset, the adoption of the term 'future economic benefits' by most of the accounting regulatory bodies in the world.

According to Checkland (1988), 'these rules are never fixed once and for all'. See also Morgan's (1980) 'radical humanist paradigm', Moore's (1991) 'critical legal studies/critical accounting' approach and Marsden and Littler's (1996) 'social constructionist paradigm' for similar organisational, legal/accounting and marketing viewpoints, respectively. It follows that if the perceptions and interpretations change, maybe because society is perceived to have changed, then there may also be a case for changing the accounting rules. For example, in the first part of the twentieth century, software, biotechnology, telecommunications, genetic engineering, and so on, were all virtually non-existent and yet today they represent potentially huge and sustainable sources of wealth.

In communicating their view of reality, accountants effectively construct that reality for themselves and for everyone who would use the financial information they produce. They typically communicate their view of business reality within recognition boundaries created by definitions and rules, such as Financial Reporting Standard 10 (FRS10) on goodwill and intangible assets (ASB 1997), which imposes a new recognition boundary on what may be capitalised and disclosed as an intangible asset. See Llewellyn's (1994) article 'Managing the boundary' for a broader exposition on boundaries. Those definitions and rules then become the accepted view of reality because of the accountants' dominance in financial matters. For as Meyer (1983) states, 'Organisational researchers have endless theoretical debates on what the boundaries are or whether there are any: the accountants settle the matter by definition, and acquiring boundaries means, for an organisation, acquiring reality.' For example, it does not matter that United Biscuits plc should after many years of capitalising brands as assets suddenly in 1998 cease to disclose brand assets on the balance sheet. The decision not to recognise and disclose brand assets is according to an FRS10 regulation rather than according to their nature as assets. Of course, such changes leave the accounting profession open to criticism from those who have a different view of business reality. These include charges by marketers as to restrictive recognition tests:

By keeping brands off the balance sheet and dismissing the claims of marketing concerning the fruits of its labour, the accounting profession succeeds in preserving its own reputation for integrity, at the expense of the integrity of marketing. ... Effective regulation depends on reliable information, and in this accounting is inevitably constrained by the uncertainties of the world which it represents. But perhaps it does not illustrate how accounting can misuse the power it gains from control of financial reporting, when the recognition tests which its applies are too restrictive. (Oldroyd 1994)

The accountants also appear to be 'out of line' with the legal profession. For example, internet domain names are recognised as legally defensible brands, the asset worth of which is not capitalised on most balance sheets (*Accountancy Age*, 1 April 1999, p. 11). However, from a legal viewpoint they can be regarded as valuable pieces of property in a similar way to most tangible assets. Consequently, I examine in this chapter why the accounting profession's view of brand assets, and related goodwill, is different from the legal view of them. This is entirely consistent with the legalist approach espoused in Part One. I look briefly at the legal literature in respect of the separable nature of brand assets and use deductive reasoning to expose the differences between the two professions' views towards them. It is a necessary first step in order to advance the case for accounting asset recognition of brand assets on the legally separable basis explained earlier in this book. Secondly, it is necessary because of the mutually authoritative influence that accounting standards, customs and practices, case law and statutes have on each profession and the consequential need for clarity of understanding. Finally, I will address the need for a definition of brand assets within the revised asset recognition boundary.

Brands tend to sustain their existence within an organised, economically developed, social context. Within this context, as social mechanisms such as an organised media and legal systems are diminished, so too is the existence of a brand similarly diminished. For example, brand attributes, such as name awareness (Aaker 1991), rely substantially on multimedia channels of communication. Also the ability to prevent copying or corruption of a related brand image relies on statute and/or access to the courts. By extension, the recognition of brands as assets, brand assets, relies on another social mechanism, namely, accounting systems. Specifically, by definition and regulation, such as those created by the UK Accounting Standards Board (ASB) or by accounting group custom and practice. Since no specific brand asset reporting standard currently exists, the accounting group custom and practice has tended to develop around the notion of either extracting and separately capitalising brand assets from purchased goodwill or, more commonly, leaving them hidden as part of purchased goodwill. It is therefore important to address the nature of goodwill again prior to any consideration being given to the separable recognition of brand assets.

There are some early accounting studies that attempt to define the nature of goodwill. It is a study that is necessary if one regards the definition/recognition of the nature of an asset, including brand assets, as a prerequisite to their measurement/valuation. Nelson (1953, p. 491) views goodwill as 'about as fickle as the human nature of which it is an aspect'. However, he argues that it may comprise customer lists, organisation costs, costs of development, *trademarks, trade names* and *brands*, secret processes and formulas, patents, copyrights, licences, franchises and superior earnings. Catlett and Olsen (1968, p. 18) argued that, 'No list of all or nearly all the factors and conditions contributing to goodwill is possible, a fact which is itself indicative of the nature of goodwill.' They, nevertheless, list the following goodwill attributes: superior management team, outstanding sales manager or organisation, weak competitor management, effective advertising, secret manufacturing processes, good labour relations, outstanding credit rating, top-flight training programmes, high standing in the community, favourable company associations, strategic location, discovered talents or resources, favourable tax conditions and favourable government regulation.

Tearney (1973, p. 44–45) argues that the term 'goodwill is an old term that has outlived its usefulness. It conveys absolutely no information to financial statement users about the underlying assets acquired.' He identifies a number of 'hidden assets' within goodwill: patents, licences, designs, unique engineering staff, *trademarks*, high product quality, good customer relations, personnel skills and marketing channels. Finally, Falk and Gordon (1977) identify the following characteristics related to goodwill: increasing short-run cash flow (cluster A), stability (cluster B), human factor (cluster C) and exclusiveness (cluster D), which includes access to technology and *brand names*. A number of goodwill attributes are common to each of the studies. In particular, it can be seen that three of the four studies identify brand names or trademarks as a constituent element of goodwill. It can be seen from these early accounting studies that the authors are, in the main, sceptical about the nature of goodwill but at least, unlike more recent accounting studies, they were prepared to recognise what they believed may be its constituent nature, inclusive of brands and trademarks.

THE LEGAL PERSPECTIVE

The asset recognition basis used by accountants is legally determined, mainly contractually. However, it is entirely feasible to extend this legal basis to include other forms of recognition such as those determined by case law or statute, for example, under the Trade Marks Act 1994. I look at that possibility here.

The legal offence of 'passing off' is to protect the proprietary interest a business has in its name, marks and get-up. The proprietary interest is separate from the right of ownership in trademarks and is widely known as the goodwill of the business. With regard to the tort of passing off, Justice Mummery states in *Associated Newspapers plc v Insert Media Ltd*:

> That tort has been developed for the protection of property which exists not in a particular name, mark or style, but in an established business, commercial or professional reputation or goodwill. Those terms embrace the enjoyment of custom and business connection, popularity and good name, and indeed, all that attracts favour and business to a particular concern and to the goods and services which it supplies. That form of property may be damaged in a number of ways by a wide variety of factual misrepresentations. (1990, 1 WLR 900–8)

It is interesting to observe Justice Mummery's attempt to address the fickle nature of goodwill along the lines of the early accounting recognition studies, above. For a valid action in passing off, the goodwill must exist, it must be misrepresented and damage caused thereby. This was affirmed in the case of *Reckitt & Colman Products v Borden Inc.* (1990, RPC 341)—the *Jiff Lemon* case. Goodwill was treated as something distinct from a brand name or trademark even though in accounting terms the latter is typically to be subsumed within goodwill. This distinction was restated by Justice Millett in *Harrods Ltd v Harrodian School Ltd* (1996, RPC 697): 'The property which is protected by an action of passing off is not the plaintiff's proprietary right in the name or get-up which the defendant has misappropriated but the goodwill and reputation of his business.'

Yet despite this apparent distinction, if it can be shown that by debasing a brand name the goodwill is likely to suffer damage, then an action in passing off will succeed, e.g. the *Lego* case and the *Champagne* case: *Lego Systems Aktieselskab v Lego Lemelstrich Ltd* (FSR. 641, 1983) and *Taittinger SA v Allbev Ltd* (1993, FSR 641). In the case of *Glaxo plc v Glaxowellcome Ltd* (1996, FSR 388) the defendant registered the Glaxowellcome name before the newly merged company of Glaxo plc and Wellcome plc was able to do so. He never intended to trade under the name and therefore there was no 'damage to the goodwill' requirement necessary for an action in passing off. Nevertheless, Justice Lightman said, 'The court will not countenance any such pre-emptive strike of registering companies with names where others have the goodwill in those names.' A similar stance and injunctive remedy was adopted in response to a pre-emptive strike in registering internet domain names; see *Harrods v UK Network Services Ltd* (1997, 4 EIPR D-106). Similarly, the defendants were unlikely to do harm to the goodwill of those companies they had registered as domain names but nevertheless the courts regarded this as passing off (Rose 1998; Anson 1998).

Murray (1997) says that 'we may be seeing the creation of a new tort which is much wider than the well-policed, well-understood tort of passing off. Indeed, it is reflective of a general tort of unfair competition.' Walsh (1998, p. 55) argues that a law of unfair competition seems the most practical way forward for this jurisdiction. Likewise, Meyer-Rochow (1998), in referring to another domain name piracy case, *Marks & Spencer plc v One In A Million* (28 November 1997, unreported), concludes:

> It is possible that the One In A Million decision will in future enable passing off to provide a remedy in a range of situations where it appears that defendant is 'unfairly' exploiting another's goodwill or reputation, even where no direct harm is committed by the defendant or apprehended by the plaintiff. This would make the remedy of passing off applicable in a wide range of circumstances far beyond that to which it has been applied in the past.

To summarise so far, firstly, brands appear to have no legal linkage to goodwill other than where damage to a brand 'passed off' simultaneously damages the goodwill of a business. Secondly, the legal profession shares some difficulty with the accounting profession in defining the nature of goodwill. However, goodwill appears from the above information to refer to customer-related attributes such as business reputation and enjoyment of custom rather than any accounting suggestion that it may also embrace hidden legally determined assets such as patents, copyright or trademarked brands. Another way of looking at it is that the legal profession is able to distinguish between customer-related capital and structural capital. This gives the legal profession the scope to consider within customer-related capital the more esoteric and distinguishing aspects of a brand, rather than just its trademark, such as brand loyalty, perceived quality and whether any damage has occurred to them. The accounting profession, on the other hand, makes no such distinction in the application of its current definitions and rules. Goodwill, brands and many other intangible assets merge within the generic heading of goodwill on the balance sheet. A couple of features flow from this distinction. Structural capital, unlike customer-related capital, possesses an artefact and typically a legally separable identity, such as that associated with a trademarked brand. Secondly, this legally separable identity can arise quite separately from the goodwill acquired as part of a transaction for the purchase of a business.

The legal basis for the recognition of brands is that of a brand's legally separable identity. For as Heigh (1997, p. 44) states: 'Brands are generally separable from the product manufacturing capacity with which they are associated. ... Brands are specific pieces of legal property. They can be sold, transferred or licensed quite separately from the related product manufacturing capacity. If properly registered and managed, brands can also have an infinite life.' The reference to brands as legal property means that they may be legally protected; that is, brands can have a legally separable identity as items of property or assets. In the UK, recognition is principally by two methods: registration under the Trade Marks Act 1994, and the common law version of it, the tort of passing off (see earlier). The difference between trademark infringement and passing off is highlighted by *United Biscuits (UK) Ltd v Asda Stores Ltd* (Chancery Division, 18 March 1997)—the *Penguin* case:

> The Puffin packaging and get-up was deceptively similar to those of Penguin, the action for passing off therefore succeeded. However, the registered word mark Penguin was held to be sufficiently dissimilar to the Puffin word sign so as to defeat the trademark infringement claim. ... For the purpose of passing off, the packaging and get-up as a whole are considered in order to decide the question of deception. However, under trademark infringement only the similarity between the actual registered mark (whether word, pictorial or both) and their look-alike equivalent can be compared in order to determine the likelihood of confusion. (Tracey 1998, p. 18)

In contrast, it matters little to accountants whether brands have a legally separable identity or that certain internally created brand assets are capable of producing future economic benefits. If, according to the accounting definition of an asset, the related transactions or events cannot be determined or they are missing then they tend not to be recognised within the accounts, for example, the Penguin brand. Contrast this situation with the legal position regarding the earlier *Penguin* case. Penguin is a long-standing, popular, international brand of considerable value and whether or not it was purchased or internally created by United Biscuits plc is immaterial to the legal recognition and defence of this property/asset. It is recognisable as an asset by nature, a legally determined and separable nature, not according to some accounting rule.

The consequence of erecting the current transactions or events boundary is that it may fail to capture enough information to portray an acceptable picture of a perceived economic reality. The picture is always incomplete, a fact not lost on the US Financial Accounting Standards Board (FASB) during the 1980s in its pursuit of a conceptual framework for accountancy. However, what accountants should determine is how much distortion in the picture is acceptable, particularly if one believes that intangible assets are of increasing importance:

> The financial statements of a business enterprise can be thought of as a representation of the resources and obligations of an enterprise and the financial flows into, out of, and within the enterprise. ... Just as a distorting mirror reflects a warped image of the person standing in front of it or just as an inexpensive loudspeaker fails to reproduce faithfully the sound that went into the microphone or onto the phonograph records, so a bad model gives a distorted representation of the system that it models. The question that accountants must face continually is how much distortion is acceptable. (FASB 1980, para 76)

One suspects that the level of distortion, particularly in respect of internally created assets, is becoming increasingly problematic for the accounting profession. This is a point worth exploring further by looking at alternative ways in which recognition of an asset could take place other than on the basis of transactions or events.

(1) Some common economic assets

Common lands: forestry, harvesting, grazing, etc.
Atmospheric gases: nitrogen, oxygen, etc.
Sea water: minerals, fish, cooling, dumping, etc.

(2) Some separable assets

'Internally created' trademarked brands, research patents, registered
    designs, copyrighted software, books, music and films
Extracted mineral deposits
Animal semen and horticultural seeds

(3) Some 'transaction or event' assets

Purchased brands, software, patents, designs, films
Other fixed assets

Figure 7.1 Asset categories

This is now briefly considered within the three broad asset categories shown in Figure 7.1:

- *Common economic assets* refer to all assets capable of producing wealth. In this category there are also assets which are uniquely common; that is, they have no separable identity attributable to any particular business entity, nor are they the result of a transaction or event but they can nevertheless be used to produce wealth, for example, the atmospheric nitrogen used by fertiliser companies.
- *Separable assets* are assets which can, if required, exist separately from the other assets of a business and which are often capable of being used to produce wealth in a variety of business situations. The separability of an asset is evidenced by being capable of transfer, physically and/or legally, between parties; a feature which incidentally appears to be lacking in respect of goodwill. A separable asset can exist irrespectively of whether it was purchased or not; that is, it is a feature of its nature rather than a business transaction.
- *Transaction- or event-based assets* are assets which are recognised usually as a result of a purchase or where a legal obligation arises such as a 'legal judgement' debtor. Transaction- or event-based recognition typically establishes a date, item and amount.

The examples in Figure 7.1 are not mutually exclusive since it is possible to move or repeat individual examples upwards (3-2-1) but not downwards (1-2-3) between categories. For example, common grazing land (category 1) is not a separable item to a business (category 2), nor the product of a transaction or event (category 3).

Similarly, internally created trademarked brands (category 2) are not the product of a transaction or event (category 3), but they have economic capabilities (category 1) such as the Coca-Cola brand. At present, only category 3 assets tend to be included on the balance sheet. The argument presented in this book is that the asset recognition trigger should now be extended to include category 2 and 3 assets. Both categories are legally determined, e.g. the statutory trademark registration of internally created brands and the contractual recognition of purchased brands, except that category 3 assets usually possess an original cost whereas category 2 assets require an independent valuation.

The definition and recognition of brand assets within a revised boundary is based on 'legal separability' rather than 'transactions or events'. If, according to the asset definition, recognition of an asset is restricted by the imposition of a transaction or event boundary, then consideration should be given either to similarly restricting the scope of the definition of a brand asset or to removing or changing the boundary in both definitions. The debate is then a question of priorities. I have already argued in Part One that changing the boundary is a necessary prerequisite to the recognition of increasingly important internally created assets, such as brand assets.

Any proposed boundary changes can be included in a new definition of a brand asset, which ideally should also try to accommodate the existing definitions of a brand from the marketing literature and the existing definitions of an asset from the accounting literature. In this latter respect the definition of a brand asset would be constitutive; that is, there would be constructs underpinning its definition which are similar to those underpinning the definition of a brand and the definition of an asset. The first sentence of the new brand asset definition (below) is clearly constitutive. It defines what a brand is and, as an asset, what it does—produce wealth. The second sentence introduces the legal boundary within which recognition of a brand asset can take place. It is based on the notion of separability as discussed in Part One. It is this latter aspect which is examined first.

DEFINITION OF A BRAND ASSET

A brand asset is a name and/or symbol (a design, a trademark, a logo) used to uniquely identify the goods or services of a seller from those of its competitors, with a view to obtaining wealth in excess of that obtainable without a brand. A brand asset's unique identity is secured through legal recognition which firstly protects the seller from competitors who may attempt to provide similar goods and/or services, and secondly enables it to exist as an entity in its own right and therefore to be capable of being transferred independently of the goods and/or services to which it was originally linked.

There is nothing particularly new about the first sentence; consider the definitions in Figure 7.2. It is the second sentence which offers the opportunity for brand asset recognition to break free from the existing recognition boundary and also its existing attachment to purchased goodwill. Let us consider it now.

- A brand is a name, term, sign, symbol or design, or combination of them which is intended to identify the goods or services of one seller to differentiate them from those of competitors. (Kotler 1980)
- A name, term, design, symbol, or any other feature that identifies one seller's good or service as distinct from those of other sellers. A brand may identify one item, a family of items, or all items of that seller. (Bennett 1988)
- A brand is a recognised name associated with a product, which projects an image to the consumer such that he or she rates the product associated with the brand higher than other comparable products. (Mainz and Mullen 1989)
- A brand is a name, symbol, design or mark that enhances the value of a product beyond its functional purpose. (Farquhar 1989)

Figure 7.2   Definitions of a brand

REVISED RECOGNITION CRITERIA

A way of recognising something which cannot be visually or tangibly recognised, is to establish some criteria for recognition which take authority by becoming acceptable to society as a whole. Recognition would then become 'context specific': it would rely on society decreeing what should become recognisable as an intangible asset, with authority being given usually through law and practice. It therefore becomes a legal abstraction which takes on a unique physical form through supporting documentation. For example, a trademark, which is intangible by nature, can be given recognition through statutory registration. A definition of a trademark is that 'words, designs, letters, numerals, shape of goods or packaging ... [are] capable of being represented graphically which is capable of distinguishing goods or services of one undertaking from those of other undertakings' (UK Trade Marks Act 1994).

Brand assets comprise more than just trademarks (such as name awareness, perceived quality) but the advantage that the latter have over the former is that their legal registration and documentation become a partial but physical surrogate for the missing intangible resource. This basis for recognising brand assets provides a higher degree of certainty as to their existence than other brand attributes such as brand loyalty and quality. Additionally, the legal identity of trademarks accords to brand assets other attributes normally associated with physical assets which would not otherwise be present, namely 'separability' and 'exchangeability' (see below). Trademarks are therefore able to offer a vehicle for the acceptance by accountants of the recognition of brands and, more importantly, of their inclusion on the balance sheet as assets, independently of purchased goodwill.

It may be argued that a trademark can never be regarded as a surrogate for a brand asset. However, compare some of the definitions of a brand in Figure 7.2 and the opening lines of my own definition of a brand asset to the definition of a trademark and observe the similarities between them. My aim is to provide a basis, in this case a legal basis, for recognition of brand assets which a few in the accounting profession have already shown they are prepared to accept on the balance sheet. The approach is one step at a time: first, break the link between brand assets and the transaction-based recognition of purchased goodwill by establishing separable legal grounds for a brand asset through a trademark, and then strengthen the process of recognition through further research into the more abstract brand attributes such as brand loyalty, brand awareness and perceived quality.

Implicit in the Figure 7.2 definitions of a brand is the notion that a brand is inextricably linked to goods or services. It follows that if the goods or services are curtailed then the brand ceases to exist. Contrast this behaviour with other assets, such as a machine, which can be put to alternative uses should certain goods or services cease to exist. The machine is separable from the other assets of the business and is often capable of being used to produce future economic benefits in a variety of business situations. This concept of separability is a fundamental feature of most assets. For example, Chambers (1966) defines an asset simply as any severable means in the possession of an entity: and by 'severable' is meant that an asset 'can be converted to other means by exchange or the processes of production or which may be alienated by way of gift.'

Recognising a brand asset as a legal entity through a trademark confers on it 'separability'; that is, in legal terms at least, the brand asset can exist as an asset independently of any product. However, this raises some serious practical problems. For example, could the unique name of Lee & Perrins exist independently of the Worcester sauce to which it is linked? To examine this point further requires an extension of the separability idea to include 'exchangeability'; that is, proof of a brand asset's separability is evidenced by the ability of the brand asset to be transferred between products and services (such as Disney films to Disney shops and products) or by being sold (such as the purchase of the use of the Cadbury brand name by Premier Brands plc). It is a fundamental aspect of a trademark, from which brand assets could be developed, that it is 'adapted of itself, standing on its own feet' (Bainbridge 1994). As a consequence, there would appear to be stronger grounds for the 'separable' balance sheet inclusion of brand assets than for goodwill. However, much of the current accounting debate on this issue is focused on goodwill since, at present, the existence of goodwill tends to be a prerequisite to any consideration being given to the separate existence of brand assets. Let us look more closely at the first sentence of the brand asset definition.

A brand is a name and/or symbol

Adolf Hitler is a well-known name and Auschwitz stands as a symbol of man's inhumanity. Whilst both name and symbol would certainly make the goods or services to which they were associated unique, it seems unlikely that either one of them would secure brand-related future economic benefits. A brand is therefore not just any unique name or symbol since its purpose is to engender in the minds of consumers a favourable attitude towards specific branded goods or services in terms of an increased propensity to purchase and repeat purchase some seller's goods instead of a competitor's goods. This is an attitude which in the minds of consumers can eventually become so strong that the name and/or symbol can stand independently of, or be transferable from, the goods or services to which they were originally linked, for example, Adidas cosmetics derived from Adidas sportswear. 'Favourable consumer attitude' is a very imprecise phrase which Aaker's (1991) brand equity definition has addressed in terms of brand loyalty, name awareness, perceived quality, etc. This is an area in which further research is required so that the brand can firstly become distinguishable from other names' and/or symbols (other than in terms of legal recognition) and secondly be verifiable; that is, one is able to quantify the strength and longevity of the favourable attitude. The definition that 'a brand is a name and/or symbol' is therefore incomplete pending further research into this area so that ultimately it can be extended to include the words 'distinguishable from other names and/or symbols in terms of' after it.

Used to uniquely identify the goods or services of a seller from those of its competitors

The association between a brand and a type of product or service can often be a strong one, for example, Jaguar and motor cars. However, it is the brand, not necessarily the product or service, that is unique. So, for example, a number of woollen jumpers may look, feel and in fact be the same but one can be distinguished from the others because it alone bears the unique Woolmark. A brand's uniqueness does not always have to depend on measures such as legal recognition of a trademark, but without them copying may be adopted by competitors.

With a view to obtaining future economic benefits

I have adopted here part of the accounting asset definition, which was criticised in Part One, until such time as the definition is changed; that is, until accountants decide what measurement method to adopt and the time frame in which to account, other than the current multiple approach.

In excess of those obtainable without a brand

A way of establishing the 'excess' from a branded product is to compare its returns to the returns from a similar generic product. However, this method could not be included in the above definition of a brand asset because sometimes a comparable generic product simply does not exist. The result is a definition which explains how the excess is to be derived but leaves unanswered the question as to how the excess is to be measured. The issue of measurement is addressed now.

BRAND VALUATION METHODS AND THEIR WEAKNESSES

Price premium method

The price premium method seeks to determine the excess or premium revenue of a brand by deducting the income of an unbranded competing product from the income of a comparable branded product. A number of assumptions are made with regard to market growth, market shares, inflation, etc., using the excess or premium as the baseline from which to establish cash flows for discounting purposes. Several difficulties arise with this method:

- There is subjectivity in cash flow construction and in selecting an appropriate discount rate.
- There may be no unbranded product that is comparable to the branded product being valued. Lee & Perrins sauce, for example, is a unique product.
- The method concentrates on price, thus it ignores cost and other commercial factors such as manufacturing economies of scale from a high-volume brand.

Earnings valuation method

The earnings valuation method seeks to apply a prudent price/earnings (P/E) multiplier or similar multiplier to a brand's profits. Typically, such profits are identified after eliminating the profits from any unbranded product produced in parallel to the branded product and also any profits from assets that do not contribute to the brand's strength. Several difficulties arise with this method:

- It is hard to select a truly representative baseline year for brand-related profits on which the multiplier is then to be applied.
- There is an underlying and perhaps unjustified assumption that P/E multiples of brand-related profits can be valued in the same way as the business as a whole.
- Multipliers that rely on an assessment of key marketing metrics such as a brand's strength typically use a highly subjective point-scoring system.
- Multipliers are of limited usefulness if there is difficulty in extracting a brand's profits in the first place.

Royalty payments method

The royalty payments method requires the determination of royalty income from the licensing out of a brand or trademark. This provides an amount on which either a discounted cash flow or multiplier can subsequently be applied. The principal difficulty is whether royalties are an effective surrogate for brand-related premiums.

Market value method

Establishing a market value assumes that a market exists. The value depends on many unknown variables, not the least of which is whether one is valuing an asset at entry prices, current market prices or exit prices. Where the brand is being sold, willingly or otherwise, the realisable value depends on the circumstances of the sale such as a competitive bidding situation. Where the brand is being acquired, it is usually valued by reference to the replacement costs involved in creating similar brand loyalty, brand awareness, and so on. Costs derived under this method are highly subjective. There is no doubt, for example, that a replacement Microsoft brand would be expensive, but until it is actually undertaken there is no way of calculating the required sum of money.

Original/historic cost method

This involves the aggregation of expenditure linked to a brand. It is obviously not a problem where a brand is purchased separately from the other assets of a business or where its value is separately identified within a contract. However, an obvious dilemma in other circumstances is the isolation of costs specific to the brand alone. The selective capitalisation of brand-related costs incurred and expensed perhaps decades ago cannot be reconciled with a balance sheet that purports to represent the aggregation of costs not yet charged to the profit and loss account rather than those that have already been expensed.

SUBJECTIVITY AT EVERY STAGE

It is clear from the above brief review of the main brand valuation methods that there is subjectivity at every stage of the valuation process. Yet despite the criticisms of a valuation-based approach, Arthur Andersen (1992) states:

> Our research confirms that there are indeed methodologies for valuing intangible assets that are well understood and applied by many different types of practitioner, both in the UK and overseas. Further we believe that these methods, and the process by which they are applied, should be codified, endorsed and promulgated as professional practice standards. This will increase the acceptance of intangible asset valuations within the business community.

In contrast, the ASB argues that, because brands share the same characteristics as goodwill, brands, newspaper titles and mastheads should be treated as part of goodwill (ASB 1993, para 3.2.6). It is a view that is obviously rejected by Arthur Andersen (1994). Arthur Andersen argues that it is a question of fact that such intangibles can be and are sold without disposing of the business, that is, they are separable as per the Companies Act definition of separability. Also, whilst acknowledging that there is no generally accepted method of measurement for such assets, it is simply because standard setters have hitherto not tackled the issue.

Coopers & Lybrand (1994, pp. 108–9) states that 'many intangibles are no less separable or capable of being reliably measured than certain tangible assets. It is inherently wrong to assume that anything that is not tangible is goodwill.' Coopers & Lybrand go on to say:

> The methodology for the valuation of acquired intangibles such as licences, publishing rights and brands is highly developed, although it may need some codification to provide quality assurance, for example, through the development of valuation guide-lines. In general the methods are as robust as the methods of valuing other items such as properties, investments and pensions.

Stoy Hayward (1994, p. 412) also recognises that brands are separable assets. However, it suggests that the ASB

> should admit that, although such assets are separable, the practical difficulties of accounting for them and the degree of subjectivity which would be involved in developing such a method, make setting separate rules impracticable.

Coopers & Lybrand (1994, p. 106) would apparently disagree and states that 'as UK business is increasingly interested in the exploitation of intangibles, it is wrong to try to turn back the clock by denying their recognition in financial statements.' According to KPMG (1994, p. 253):

> Almost all purchased intangible assets will be subsumed within goodwill on the basis that it is impossible to measure the value of these assets reliably. We do not agree. We appreciate the difficulties in valuing intangible assets but do not believe that this should prevent recognition where such assets are purchased as part of a package in acquiring a business.'

Part Three
The Politics of Brand Assets

8
A process of consultation, not consensus?

The dominant power of the ASB in standard setting means that accounting standards are deeply implicated in the reproduction of values on what may be regarded as capable of disclosure in the published financial statements. Specifically, what may be disclosed as an intangible asset? The political process of standard setting often means that standards are rarely objective or neutral in their conveyance of meaning to would-be users. It is a process which usually requires a degree of consensus within it and then subsequently outside it in terms of compliance in accounting practice. Of course, as Chapter 5 showed, compliance is not always uniform. One of the reasons I suspect is that the process may not actually be one of consensus but rather one of consultation.

The reality in respect of goodwill and intangible assets is that consensus has been virtually impossible to obtain in the past. Thus, the difficult task for the ASB has been to steer its preconceptions through the troubled waters of the consultation process, knowing that at the end of the day consensus on the validity of FRS10 would be for many silently missing or reluctantly accepted as inevitable. In this regard, offering a hybrid accounting option of 'capitalise/amortise and capitalise/review' in FRS10 was a politically astute move which left many in the profession feeling they could reluctantly live with it.

On pragmatic grounds, the ASB is to be congratulated. However, as this book seeks to show, I have serious reservations about the process on conceptual grounds. For example, Christopher Nunn is

> well aware of the enormous effort which the ASB has put in to try to formulate proposals which will obtain consensus support. However, my perception is that if such a consensus is obtained it will be a fragile one, based partly on exhaustion with debating the topic and partly on a feeling amongst preparers that the important issue is to secure the ability to capitalise intangibles, particularly brands, and that the goodwill proposals, while arousing little positive enthusiasm and receiving quite a lot of objection, are sufficiently flexible to be lived with and finessed as necessary. I do not think this is a satisfactory platform from which to proceed. I therefore find myself in the perhaps politically incorrect position of having to say that so far as the goodwill proposals are concerned the emperor, in the form of the ASB, has rather flimsy clothes. (ASB 1995z, pp. 36–37)

In this chapter I undertake a partial examination of the political process leading up to the implementation of FRS10. I have used the responses to the ASB's public hearings as a source of information for this examination. I dip occasionally into the responses to the discussion paper and working paper but as I want to leave them together with the issue of valuation methods for another book, they will only be touched on briefly. I have chosen the public hearings rather than the earlier responses to the discussion and working papers because the spoken word rather than the written word is less guarded in its delivery. In other words, it is more revealing even if at times the structure of the sentences become muddled.

Why undertake this examination? I hope in this book I have put forward a reasonable case for the disclosure of brand assets by arguing for a broadening of the existing asset recognition boundary on conceptual and pragmatic grounds so that more intangible assets are captured within it. However, as the Ranks Hovis McDougall case showed in 1988, if accountants wish to disclose brand assets, they can bend the rules to do so. But they choose not to do so. An examination such as this one therefore reveals some important insights into why they choose not to do so. The subject matter is perhaps only relevant to accountants, so my apologies to the non-accountants reading this chapter and the next one too.

Throughout this chapter and the next you will see references to names which will be the interviewees, together with the following panel members: Messrs Tweedie, Goeltz, Jones, Cook, Whittington, Wild, Hinton, Garner and Ms Kennedy. Most of the responses were in respect of goodwill rather than brands. However, by now the reader will be well aware of the close relationship between the two and therefore the subject matter is still relevant to the focus of this book.

ASB PUBLIC HEARINGS HELD 26–28 SEPTEMBER 1995

The responses are structured across two chapters into the following groupings. Chapter 8 addresses the national and international scene—allowable accounting methods, the nature of goodwill and intangible assets, the linkage to the Statement of Principles in respect of definition of an asset, and Chapter 9 addresses the linkage to the Statement of Principles in respect of transactions/matching and valuation-based approaches to intangibles and the role of separability. The references will refer to ASB 1995x, 1995y or 1995z, sequentially, for each of the three days of the public hearings.

THE NATIONAL AND INTERNATIONAL SCENE: ALLOWABLE ACCOUNTING METHODS

In his opening comments, Sir David Tweedie mapped the political milestones since the introduction of SSAP22 in 1984 (ASB 1995x, pp. 3–5). The International Accounting Standards Committee proposed the international banning of the reserve write-off approach to purchased goodwill. This prompted the ASC in 1990 to introduce ED47 and ED52, which proposed the international approach of the capitalisation and amortisation of purchased goodwill and other intangible assets. Sir David highlighted the hostile approaches of the vast majority of respondents towards ED47 and ED52. This left the ASC with a dilemma that was passed on to its successor body, the ASB: 'So the Board was faced with this opposition to the compulsory amortisation and the fact that internationally there was no support for writing off the reserves' (ASB 1995x, p. 4).

The preference of Sir David Tweedie for the international approach of capitalisation was demonstrated by the following comment:

> Intangible assets can be recognised if the fair value can be assessed reliably, but the treatment of intangibles and goodwill are closely aligned, so there is no accounting arbitrage, there is not an advantage to call it either a brand or goodwill. Where there is a finite life, you will expect it to depreciate over that life. Where there is an indefinitely

long life, you can use an impairment test: a very full one if you are not amortising and a reduced one if, in fact, you are amortising in any event. We assume, though it can be rebutted, that goodwill does not last more than 20 years in line with the international standard. (ASB 1995x, pp. 4–5)

It was a point repeated again on the final day of the hearings (ASB 1995z, p. 5).

The proposition (supported by Sir David's comment) is that goodwill and other intangibles are both to be capitalised and it does not matter whether that is separately or as one under the umbrella of purchased goodwill. There is no mention of reserve write-off at all here. What is clear is that the asset status (or investment status, if one dubiously wishes to distinguish between the two descriptions) of goodwill, is taken for granted and all that remains is a determination of its life expectancy. However, we need to go back a step because the asset status of goodwill is unproven and therefore any assertion as to no arbitrage is also unproven. Even more so if intangibles, such as brands, patents and licences, are regarded as assets and goodwill is not, or where part of goodwill is actually shown to be an overpayment, an expense. That is, where it should be written off rather than being capitalised. Under such circumstances arbitrage can occur legitimately and, it can be argued, makes 'bottom-line' sense where certain intangibles are capitalised without amortisation.

There is also the conceptual point of disclosing the real intangible wealth creators in a business rather than a dubious generic goodwill heading. John Cook (ASB 1995z, p. 92) believes purchased goodwill should be charged immediately through the profit and loss (P&L) account—what he refers to as 'the biggest of baths'. It is a position I would support in respect of the residue left after capitalising all other intangible assets. In his conclusion Sir David Tweedie responded: 'Thank you very much, John. I said at the beginning there are three ways of dealing with goodwill, now there are clearly four [he was referring to P&L write-off]' (ASB 1995z, p. 100). It was meant humorously but it actually hides a serious observation. The opening comments of Sir David Tweedie on each of the three days of the public hearings assumed only three methods.

The failure to acknowledge even the possibility of P&L write-off suggests some predisposition towards capitalisation rather than write-off approaches to goodwill. Mr Hinton (ASB 1995z, p. 96), for example, referred to Mr Cook's suggestion as 'somewhat oppressive'. Sir David (ASB 1995z, p. 99) indicated that shareholders might be 'rather cross' at the wild fluctuations in reported year-end losses in the year of acquisition and the subsequent year-end post-acquisition profits. The reality, however, is that regardless of such pragmatic considerations it is a legitimate approach to purchased goodwill, particularly if some or all of purchased goodwill is simply an overpayment.

Sir David Tweedie's preferences for international comparability are highlighted by the following exchange with Mr Chitty:

> The other thing that I would like to ask you about is that you mentioned that we should not really follow the International Standards Committee and that we should ignore the external situation. That is almost counter to the Board's philosophy in a way. I think that the view that the Board has been adopting is that, in fact, UK accounting should move more into the international main stream. By all means look to lead, but we should not deliberately walk in the other direction unless we genuinely think that there are special cases in the UK (fiscal cases or something like that) that change the situation here or that, in fact, we think the international proposals are wrong. (ASB 1995x, p. 32)

The international proposals remain directed towards the capitalisation and amortisation of goodwill. However, Christopher Nunn says:

> The international practice is driven by the US practice. The US practice is driven by a critical compromise when Governments threaten to intervene to prevent an accounting standard which required an immediate write-off of goodwill. This idea that the rest of the world has really cracked this thing, and got a conceptually sound answer is based on a misconception as to how the US standard actually arrived on the scene. (ASB 1995z, p. 43)

An interesting observation on the direction of international harmonisation in goodwill accounting was raised by Professor Myddleton, who referred to the earlier discussion paper response by Arthur Andersen:

> It told me something that I did not know, namely, when the Americans first set up their way of coping with goodwill, it was a compromise, quite arbitrary and so on. I had not been aware of that. It is a fair point. If we want to fall in line with other people, what they are doing may not have any particularly convincing justification. I think I agree with the implication in what you said. It would be nice if we were in line with international accounting standards, but I do not regard it as absolutely critical. (ASB 1995y, p. 63)

Mr Hinton responded:

> I think that that is very much the way in which the Board would like to harmonise and to follow international standards, but not necessarily when they have a fettered history. Just for the record, the American standard was a product not of the accounting profession, but of Congress. The accounting profession recommended immediate write off and Congress mandated, prompted by the business community, for a very long period of amortisation. I think that, quite honestly, that is a very valid reason for the Board taking up a different approach to the present international standards. (ASB 1995y, p. 63)

Interestingly, Sir David Tweedie, said:

> The basis for the IASC standard was an American standard which even predated the Financial Accounting Standards Board in about 1970 and it was at a time when goodwill in the United States was about one per cent of net assets (ASB 1995x, p. 3)

What can we conclude from this, so far? The UK position on the capitalisation of purchased goodwill may be based on a follow-my-US-leader approach to standard setting. If correct, capitalisation is based on almost entirely pragmatic considerations rather than any conceptual basis as to the status of goodwill as an asset. Let us examine this assertion further.

THE NATURE OF GOODWILL AND INTANGIBLE ASSETS

The opening comments of the chairman, Sir David Tweedie (ASB 1995x, p. 3), on the first day of the public hearings were interesting in that they focused on the choice of accounting method. There was no attempt to ground these methods on any conceptual basis as to the status of purchased goodwill as an asset or not. So, for example, there was no mention of the possibility that purchased goodwill was simply the result of a mismatch of measurement methods, cost and fair values, or that some or all of it might be an overpayment. Similarly, at the beginning of the second day of the hearing, Sir David Tweedie said, 'As far as goodwill is concerned, I am sure that you are all aware that there are only three different ways in which you can deal with it' (ASB 1995y, p. 3). To repeat, none of these ways entertained the possibility that some or all of goodwill is an expense to be charged through the P&L account. Chris Pearce, for example, said:

> I believe, in fact, that we would probably much assist the discussion of the treatment of goodwill if we actually gave it another name and called it say, 'difference on consolidation' because that is really what it is. Particularly goodwill arising on consolidation. In any review it is important to remember that goodwill is not an asset ... [and it follows] that amortising goodwill does not reflect underlying economic reality. (ASB 1995z, pp. 7–8)

Mr Hinton, for example, commented on the lack of conceptual support for the asset status of goodwill in the following terms: 'In fact, the submissions to both the ASC and the ASB have been very, very light on identifying what we actually have in goodwill' (ASB 1995y, p. 88). He asked Professor Page 'whether he thought goodwill is exactly the same assets as all the others or whether its characteristics and its nature are actually identified as something really quite distinct.' The professor replied:

> I think that in both frameworks, the decision-usefulness framework and the accountability framework, goodwill is an asset. In the decision-usefulness framework an asset is simply something that enables you to earn cash flows in future. Goodwill seems to do that just as a bicycle or any other kind of asset within a business. In an accountability framework, assets are items in which the management of the enterprise has invested resources and for which they remain accountable. Goodwill satisfies that definition of an asset just as well. (ASB 1995y, p. 88)

Christopher Nunn, in contrast, said:

> Identifiable intangibles and purchased goodwill are not identical twins. Intangible assets which can be identified and measured are indeed assets which should be capitalised and amortised. Purchased goodwill, to quote the Working Paper, is an anomaly, representing nebulous intangible benefits that do not satisfy the definition and recognition requirements of identifiable assets. I agree with this view that purchased goodwill is anomalous and nebulous. To continue with the long abstract adjectives it is a residual and ephemeral balance which results from a transaction and, often, from share values at a particular instant in time, and thereafter loses its significance. Because it is an inseparable part of the business and the factors which may contribute to it cannot be valued, it only has relevance in the context of the value of the business as a whole. The role of accounting is to provide information about the separable resources which are used to produce earnings, and not to seek and record and track the total value of the business. (ASB 1995z, p. 34)

Three issues are important here. Firstly, separability has a central role in the asset recognition process, a process which focuses initially on resource recognition. Secondly, intangibles are separable, whilst goodwill is inseparable from the other assets of a business. Thus, following on from the first point, goodwill is not an asset and it is consequently wrong to treat them both as 'identical twins'. Thirdly, whilst purchased goodwill is transaction based in accordance with the UK accounting definition of an asset, the transaction produces little substance—a 'residual and ephemeral balance'.

In considering the nature of goodwill, some respondents thought of it in terms of synergistic gains where two businesses are combined. At the beginning of Chapter 6, Professor Baxter refers to the value of a matched pair of porcelain figures, as opposed to their value as separable items. Mr Wild addressed Will Baxter's response to the discussion and working papers in respect of his two porcelain shepherds:

> The reason that I am saying that is that there seems to be variations in its value that can occur independently of the two statues. If you have a pair of shepherds and that takes the value from £100 each to £1,000 but then research indicates that actually they are two of a set of four, which will cost you shepherds, the value will fall back down and the two shepherds still may be worth £100 each, but the difference between them would vary, or, conversely, if they were the only two shepherds in existence and one fell and broke, you would find that there would be a transfer in value from the synergy (the difference element) to the individual shepherd. The individual shepherd is a unique shepherd and then may become worth £1,000 in his own right. That possibility of variation within the value of this difference, moving as an independent item, I accept that it is just a difference, but why does that variation not need to be treated as an asset in its own right? (ASB 1995x, p. 63)

Will Baxter replied:

> I think that the answer to all such problems is: what is the market unit? It may well bear no relationship to the price of the individual items that go into the making of that unit.

However, Mr Wild responded that the

> market unit may vary without the individual items varying, just because research has indicated that they are not a pair, they are two of four. The individual items have not varied, but the market unit has. Does that not indicate that it is something that does exist as a separate thing?

Finally, in this exchange, Will Baxter said:

> No, it just indicates that the market tastes go up and down. Partly it is a matter of the buyer's taste and partly because of the number of the items that come on to the market.

Note, from the exchange between Wild and Baxter, that the debate is measurement focused. The unproven point, which they both seem to accept, is the possibility of synergistic gains as a result of comparison of the different measurement bases. Of course, the goodwill difference may just be the result of a mismatch of measurement bases, nothing more, and what is required is actually the application of a single measurement basis so that no difference arises in the first place. That is, a market approach at £1000 or a transaction-based approach at 2 × £100, but not a comparison between the two for disclosure purposes.

David Evans advanced his idea of market goodwill (ASB 1995x, p. 91), it being the difference between book values and the current market value. However, in criticising this approach, Mr Wild drew

> a distinction between net assets as stated in a balance sheet, which will largely be historical cost, and the assessment that the market will put on the net assets if there were a transaction. You [Mr Evans] are comparing the company if there was a whole

transaction of the whole company. I think that there is a slight concern over capital-isation anyway, because that is not the amount at which the whole company would trade, but that is the accumulation of the amount at which small bundles of shares trade. Unless you accumulate those small bundles of shares and give the total value for the company, you are not putting in the market valuation. (ASB, 1995x, p. 95)

Professor Whittington clarified the point by saying that 'if you want to take a company over, you would not pay the market share price. In a takeover bid, in order to get the full value of control of the company, you have to pay much more, usually, than the on-going share price' (ASB 1995x, p. 95). Though perhaps a poor one, the comparison which could be drawn with Mr Evan's approach is what used to happen in parts of the public sector. For 364 days of the year they adopted cash-based accounting and then at the year end there was a determination of individual 'commitments' to spend or receive monies, debtors/creditors, so as to provide accruals-based year-end accounts. Similarly, it would appear with Mr Evan's approach, that transaction-cost-based accounting is largely adopted during the year and then at the year end the overall market value is determined and hence the market value goodwill balancing figure. At least with the 'cash versus accrual' approach there was linkage at the individual payment/receipt level, whereas with this approach the market value relates to goodwill alone as a market value balancing figure, at one moment only. There is apparently no similar linkage to the other assets of the business. We are not comparing like with like for all the assets of a business.

Archer states, 'I concur with the view of the Board that pure goodwill, at least, is not an asset in the normal sense. It is an emergent component and value' (ASB 1995y, pp. 69–70). He justifies this nebulous phrase in terms of Professor Baxter's synergistic returns from his 'porcelain shepherds' example: 'that is the sort of thing that goodwill is'. Likewise, he extends this rather vague statement to intangibles such as brands, what he refers to as 'quasi-goodwill'. However, the key issue here, in respect of the asset status of goodwill and quasi-goodwill, is what he alludes to in the following comment:

> I would suggest to the Board that a firm view should be taken regarding this type
> of item, quasi-goodwill, and the same accounting rules should have to be applied to
> these items (i.e. non-separable intangibles) as are applied to pure goodwill.

Specifically, it is the role of separability as a key criterion in the accounting recognition of intangibles. As my earlier chapters indicate, it is a viewpoint I would endorse, though perhaps the difference between us is that I would regard a trademarked brand as a separable asset.

A traditional accounting approach to purchased goodwill would acknowledge that one is dealing with a debit here, assets or expenses, not 'emergent components', 'under-lying investment', 'economic object' or any other description. Archer eventually refers to purchased goodwill as a 'consolidation difference' that arises because of the aggregation problem (ASB 1995y, p. 71). As a 'difference' one then needs to recognise its separable identity as an asset, or not, and then determine whether it can produce future economic benefits, or not. If the answer is no then its status as an expense is confirmed since this is the only alternative accounting treatment if one follows a traditional debit/credit, transaction-based approach to accounting. In this context, questions from Sir David Tweedie to Simon Archer such as 'Do you, too, consider goodwill to be an asset or do you relate it back to the original investment?' seem to be unnecessarily complex (ASB 1995y, p. 71). It is an asset, which includes investments, or it is an expense—take your pick!

Professor Page, for example, refers to the fact that some or all of purchased goodwill may be an overpayment and therefore it should be expensed:

> The over-payment problem: we can observe that the success of takeovers is mixed. Evidence on this is fairly sparse and not all commentators agree, but we can be sure that not all takeover bids are successful in the long term. That means that sometimes people overpay for goodwill. This is not much of a problem if goodwill is amortised, but, if the ASB adopts its decision usefulness valuation approach and people maintain goodwill, one needs to be assessing whether overpayment has occurred. One might even go so far as to say that, if stock markets are efficient, then companies are probably quite well valued before they are taken over. In the absence of strong evidence that companies achieve performance improvements in the companies that they take over, which is lacking, then bid premiums should all be written off to the profit and loss account unless there is strong evidence to the contrary. (ASB 1995y, p. 85)

According to Chris Higson, overpayments to acquire a business are endemic and it is unreasonable to expect firms that have overpaid to readily acknowledge it. He argues, from an observation of the consistency of many market-based studies, that the acquirer's share prices tend to show zero returns around takeover:

> In other words, takeover is neither a value creating nor a value destroying event for acquirers on average. This should not be a surprise because it is consistent with a highly competitive market for corporate control. Where there are economic gains to takeovers the bidding process puts them in the hands of the selling shareholders. But it has very powerful implications for the value of goodwill, because if on average there is nothing in it for the acquirers, that means that around the average would be many takeovers with positive abnormal returns for the acquirer, where the acquirer gains, and many where it loses. Indeed, my evidence suggests that if stock prices are to be believed overpayment was a significant proportion of reported goodwill in the UK in many, many cases, most notably during the merger wave period between 1986 and 1991 when levels of goodwill were very high. During this period a majority of acquiring firms experienced a decline in share price when they announced a takeover. The implication of that is that in the majority of cases goodwill was overvalued. In many cases that was quite extreme and in getting on for 20% of cases the overpayment element constituted at least half, and in some cases all of the recorded accounting goodwill. In fact, in 7% of takeovers over that period the market immediately wrote down the value of the acquiring firm by more than the total of the accounting goodwill. So we must not imagine that overpayment for goodwill is a rare event. I think it is endemic for good market reasons. (ASB 1995z, pp. 46–47)

The evidence presented by Chris Higson suggests that the overpayment element of purchased goodwill should be expensed. Of the remaining goodwill, some or all of it may contribute towards the creation of future economic benefits, but it may be so inseparable, so nebulous, so doubtful as to its 'assetness' as to be unidentifiable and therefore should also be expensed. One is then left with the possibility of extracting some identifiable intangibles, such as brands, from the remaining goodwill such that what remains thereafter may be insignificant. Of course, this presupposes in the first place that a goodwill 'difference' has economic substance and may be hiding intangible assets. The market certainly appears to value goodwill but as to what exactly, asset by asset, is being valued, that is unknown. It suggests that where intangible assets are identifiable they should be capitalised, and the remaining purchased goodwill should be written off as quickly as possible. However, this was rejected on the rather dubious grounds that the big problem with write-off, and 'I think its fatal flaw, is the loss of audit trail' (ASB 1995z, p. 50).

It was therefore surprising that Mr Higson advanced the case for amortising goodwill on what appear to be entirely pragmatic grounds, specifically:

- The goodwill debate had gone on too long and compromise was called for.
- When it is very hard to choose between two alternatives, in this case between capitalised goodwill with or without amortisation, it often means it does not matter which one is chosen.

Like many respondents to the discussion and working papers, he also regarded the impairment tests as being highly subjective. He advanced the case for capitalisation and amortisation on the basis of international harmonisation (ASB 1995z, p. 48).

To summarise this section so far, there is little evidence that the debate surrounding goodwill and intangible assets had any conceptual foundation to it, particularly in determining the asset status of purchased goodwill. There were a substantial number of concerns expressed about its assetness but, as far as I have been able to observe, no theoretical rationalisation of its assetness along the lines presented in this book. To me, this is a very serious omission. How can one propose capitalisation as a solution if one is not even sure whether one is dealing with an asset? How can one consider impairing it, whatever 'it' is? Let us look at that now.

All the responses in respect of impairment, not surprisingly, referred to the process itself. Sir David Tweedie argued that 'the responses to our discussion paper were clear cut in only one direction and that is that 70% did not like the idea of not separating intangible assets and goodwill' (ASB 1995y, p. 4). Unfortunately, it was only partially correct. They were also very clear about the impairment test process. They overwhelmingly disliked it. I assure you that the adjectives used by some of the respondents would make my comment appear tame by comparison. But that is for another book. It was interesting to note from the longitudinal survey (Chapter 5) that the overwhelming majority of companies chose to capitalise and systematically amortise goodwill. I wonder why? Could it be that the alternative approach of impairment was too unpalatable? We can now consider some of the public hearing responses to impairment but bear in mind as we go through them that they all assume there is something to impair in the first place. However, if the nature of goodwill is that it is not an asset, then there is nothing to impair. Now, that would be amusing: the emperor's new clothes are wearing out!

Mr Chitty describes the impairment reviews as a 'creative accountant's dream':

> It is quite possible, as has been said, for the figures to be fiddled. We are playing with discounted figures and we are playing with the future. It is quite easy for a finance director to justify what he wants and to sell it to his auditors. Yes, the directors will sign the representation letter; yes, the directors will sign the accounts; it may be a long time before it comes out. Equally, I am concerned about the need to invoke the true and fair view override and a lack of compatibility with the existing UK companies legislation. . . . Encouraging the use of the true and fair view override is correct where it is economically realistic, but it does encourage industry to go out and, again, look for other ways and means to invoke the override if the standard setting board are encouraging that. (ASB 1995x, p. 29)

In this regard, Mr Chitty was simply reiterating the views of the vast majority of the respondents to the discussion and working papers as to the overall subjectivity of these reviews.

There are those who argue that, in allowing the use of discounted cash flows for impairment purposes, the ASB has opened up Pandora's box in that one more measurement basis is introduced into accounting. It is a basis which is inherently subjective and one which partly justifies the approach of many intangible valuers in that such techniques are often used by them to establish valuations. Mrs Jackson argues that 'by looking at future cash flows of bought intangibles, you are, in effect, establishing a methodology which is easily used for internally generated assets' (ASB 1995x, p. 43). In reply, Sir David Tweedie said:

> Mr Damant will tell you that we are not and what we are really doing there is assessing as asset's value from its future cash flows. We are looking at the recoverable amount. It is: is the amount that you have shown there equal to its recoverable amount? If it is higher, it has to come down. It is the old cost or less argument that we use for historical cost, even current assets. It is that sort of argument. We are not saying it is the value. It is the maximum value and we would bring it down to that. It is not the value we would normally show.

Nevertheless, it does formalise a technique from a regulatory point of view which is inherently subjective. As an approach it has now been formalised in FRS11 (ASB 1998) and stands in contrast, presumably as a reliable measurement technique, to the overriding requirement within this overall process for there to be reliability of measurement based on transaction-based cost. Pandora's box has definitely been opened.

Michael Hughes expressed concern over the use of cash flows as a valid indicator of impairment:

> We also believe that the indicators of possible impairment will require some re-examination. The first indicator is linked to the cash flow, either in the current period or expected in the future. I think that generally negative cash flows are not going to be a sensible measure. They are much more likely to indicate an expanding business to which the management is committing further investment than one that is in decline. In fact, I think that in many declining businesses, the cash flow tends to be positive as they reach their demise. I think that losses or negative operating cash flows would be more appropriate indicators. (ASB 1995y, p. 40)

Professor Myddleton suggests that

> with respect to impairment, the Board does mix up, I think, two different things: (a) the original purchased goodwill and (b) the original purchased goodwill together with subsequent topping up. There is no point comparing the value of (b) with the cost of (a). For impairment purposes, it is the value of (a) at which we should be looking, that is, the current value of the original purchased goodwill. I agree with the Board that internally generated goodwill should not be capitalised. Therefore, expenditure on topping up purchased goodwill should not be capitalised. There is no justification for maintaining intact the original cost of purchased goodwill on the balance sheet since, in my view, it is a rapidly wasting asset if it is not subsequently topped up. (ASB 1995y, p. 59)

Professor Archer would perhaps express some sympathy with this view of 'topping up', expressed eloquently as 'the elixir that gives it [purchased goodwill] this longevity is actually the internally generated goodwill which is being transfused into it' (ASB 1995y, p. 69). Mr Wild subsequently confirmed:

> We probably accept your [Professor Myddleton's] argument about replacing purchased goodwill with inherent goodwill. It is an argument that has been raised by others.

...I think that your argument about the purchase inherent means that it is virtually impossible to determine an actual life for goodwill, which is what I think we meant by 'indefinite' rather than 'infinite'. Consequently, I think that, if we go your route and have amortisation over a period, the period is going to be fairly arbitrary. (ASB 1995y, p. 60)

Mr Wild then asked Professor Myddleton if the ASB's alternative approach of an impairment test had any value. In reply, Professor Myddleton offered a strict transaction-based view of accounting:

In the context of historical cost accounting, you are trying to value goodwill as you go along. That is not what I think accounts are for. It is completely inconsistent to be trying to look at a very hard-to-measure current value of purchased goodwill plus all the subsequent expenditure. All that I am interested in is writing off the cost (not the value) of purchased goodwill over a prudently short, admittedly arbitrary, period.

Professor Page also expressed concerns about the subjectivity of the impairment tests and that systematic depreciation would eventually account for a decline in asset value:

Our current practice, it seems to me, works on the basis that depreciation rates are conservative or prudent, so that, in general, for most companies, taking the fixed assets of the group, then the valuation of fixed assets is supportable. They are not impaired. There are difficulties where you come across a large asset which has suffered impairment. By and large, I think at the moment we skate round those problems and probably not too much harm comes from it, eventually depreciation will solve it. (ASB 1995y, p. 92)

Whereas the depreciation of goodwill here is a one-way decrease in value, in contrast, in respect of brands, Jeremy Pennant

feels strongly that any write down in the value of an intangible asset should be reversible. [For example] ... there have been other brands that have been repositioned or relaunched in the market place promoting a different image with startling effects and, just as importantly, an increase in their value. (ASB 1995y, p. 95)

In response to a question from Mr Wild about the implementation of arbitrary amortisation periods, Mr Pennant said that

with due deference to the people who have spoken before me, talking about a 20 year period and writing off the value of, say, a brand or trademark is not being realistic. People spoke about Johnny Walker [Johnnie Walker] earlier and the Bass Red Triangle, too, is still going strong. I would say that both those brands have probably increased in value over a period of more than 100 years. Therefore, you cannot say in real life that writing those down over a 20 year period is giving the true and fair view. (ASB 1995y, pp. 96–97)

Kevin Plummer of Guinness plc, which owns the Johnnie Walker brand, obviously agrees:

we feel that this clearly shows that certain types of intangible assets can have a very enduring value indeed [and] ... to us, therefore, compulsory amortisation of such assets is illogical in that costs are being double counted. (ASB 1995z, p. 19)

It was argued, however, that such examples were the exception that proved the rule. Mr Pennant would disagree:

> There are hundreds of thousands of trademarks that have lasted longer than 20 years.
> When you look at most of the famous brands in the world, they have increased in
> value. The famous ones about which everyone talks have been there for years and
> years and years. They are not the new ones. (ASB 1995y, p. 97)

Allister Wilson raised a concern about the field tests that were conducted by the ASB to
assess the acceptability of the impairment tests from a user perspective:

> What concerns me, and I think I am correct in saying that the sample companies
> which field tested the impairment test were 100% the brand companies. Therefore,
> it is not very surprising that you are going to get overwhelming support from the
> companies who, quite clearly, would very much like to show their brands legitimately
> as permanent assets on their balance sheets and not have to amortise them. So, it is
> very much a case of the Sunday trading debate. If you ask Sainsbury's, Tesco and
> Waitrose what they thought of Sunday trading, and then we could say 'we got 100%
> support for Sunday trading.' (ASB 1995z, p. 111)

Professor Whittington thought his comments were 'off the wall':

> I am sure the ASB has not deliberately sought just to find people who are going to
> comply with some Standard that we have not yet defined, because that is why we are
> having all the public hearings now to define the Standard. We have tried to get people
> to co-operate. Obviously the people who will co-operate are the sort of people we
> have got, the people with brands and things like that. They are the people who are
> interested in this sort of thing. (ASB 1995z, p. 115)

With respect to Professor Whittington, the excuse was a poor one and it actually validated
Allister Wilson's comments. The comment is not off the wall, because as a researcher
he knows that to pre-select a target audience which has a built-in predisposition towards
the researcher's intended outcome is poor research. I am sorry to possibly add offence to
injury but that is the way I see it too.

Remember, I said to hold in your mind the idea that some or all of purchased goodwill
may not be an asset when considering its impairment. Let us now examine that idea in
relation to the definition of an asset.

THE LINKAGE TO THE STATEMENT OF PRINCIPLES: DEFINITION OF AN ASSET

Mr Chitty firmly believed that

> goodwill and intangibles are assets. They do represent rights to future economic bene-
> fits and the best place to put them is on the balance sheet. Indeed, I believe that much
> of the support that remains for the SSAP22 preferred approach comes very simply
> from the EPS arguments. If you write it off to reserves, it does not dilute your earnings
> per share. Let us continue with the fight to get rid of reserve accounting and consign
> that to the past. (ASB 1995x, p. 28)

In contrast, Mrs Jackson said:

> Goodwill is not really an asset, it is more a cost of control. Certainly for large industrial
> companies, it is the premium that they are paying to take control of an organisation.
> (ASB 1995x, p. 41)

Sir David Tweedie responded with the following comment:

> You say that it is not an asset, but, on the other hand, we have heard Mr Chisman
> say this morning that, in fact, he could actually sell that and get the cash, because
> the asset is, is it not, the underlying asset of the investment which you are showing
> in your parent company balance sheet, and presumably you believe that it is intact,
> otherwise you would write it down and reduce your dividends?

It was a pity that Mrs Jackson did not argue her point further in that goodwill as a cost of
control may result, at times, in an overpayment. The investment, if it is one, is therefore
not intact and the write-off method is consequently appropriate in these circumstances.
The asset status point is a fundamentally important conceptual point to make because
if goodwill is not an asset then to a large extent the capitalisation approach of FRS10
becomes redundant. Instead, her reply diluted the strength of her initial argument. Let us
consider it further.

Mrs Jackson (ASB 1995x, p. 42) argued that purchased goodwill is replaced by internally generated goodwill such that it becomes indistinguishable from it. However, Sir
David Tweedie replied:

> I think that Mr Chisman would probably say to you that he did not care, because
> basically he is saying 'I have got an investment which is worth £100 million. At the
> end of five years it is still worth £100 million, so I do not care whether it is internally
> generated or purchased, I know that I can sell that and get my money back. If I start
> writing anything off, what I am going to do is to show a loss in the profit and loss
> account for something that I could, in fact, then sell and get all that loss back again,
> plus possibly more.' I think that the argument that we meet with industrialists is that
> they just do not accept the notion of internally generated goodwill replacing. They are
> just saying 'I am looking at the investment.'

Sir David Tweedie suggests, 'I do not care whether it is internally generated or purchased,
I know that I can sell that and get my money back.' An obvious response to this assertion
is, What exactly am I selling or buying? The answer is that no one in their right mind
would sell or purchase goodwill alone because, insofar as it exists as an asset, it is
inseparable from the other assets of a business. Further, the assertion that there is an
investment which is still worth £100 million five years later is a bold assumption given
the vagaries of the marketplace.

The reality is that we do not know what proportion of 'money back', if any, is
attributable to goodwill. For example, assuming goodwill is an investment, we do not
know what proportion of 'money back' is simply the result of the good or poor management of goodwill as distinct from other assets. We know that, generally speaking, something over and above the tangible assets of a business contributes to wealth creation but
we do not know what it is by nature or what proportion is simply an overpayment. Insofar
as goodwill does represent something of worth, then let that something be recognised.
And this, I would suggest, was really the point Mr Swetman alluded to in his response
to Sir David Tweedie:

> I think that again the question is whether you want to see the balance sheet as a sort
> of inventory of all assets of a company, tangible and intangible, or not, because, as I
> have indicated, there are a whole load of intangible assets that have a value that could
> be sold which you would not put on the balance sheet even after this. (ASB 1995x,
> p. 42)

This exchange was beneficial in that it not only highlighted some important recognition issues but also led on to what I think was one of the most important features of the whole debate—that the recognition of nature of the goodwill asset or investment is driven by the overriding requirement for there to be a recognisable transaction-based cost, which purchased goodwill clearly has. In other words, the £100 million (above) is measured with certainty according to a known transaction and all that remains is to decide whether to capitalise it or not. There is no conceptual reasoning as to its status as an asset because, it is suggested, if there was, then such reasoning would reasonably conclude that it is irrelevant whether an asset was purchased or internally generated. What matters is whether by nature it is an asset or not. The dominance of measurement is effectively acknowledged by Sir David Tweedie in the following comment (for 'brand' perhaps read any 'intangible asset'):

> I think that the problem that we would really have is the fact that it is quite clear that you must have an internally generated brand as equally valuable as a purchased brand. The problem is the reliability of measuring that, which is why we were asking our speakers earlier about reliability. We do not traditionally in accounting bring assets in if we cannot measure them reliably. (ASB 1995x, p. 42)

Sir David Tweedie, in response to the Davies brothers, said:

> I noticed in your submission that you did not like the words 'economic meaning in the balance sheet'. I did not like you saying that you did not like 'economic meaning in the balance sheet', because that, I think, is what we are actually trying to bring in, something acting as a signal and actually meaning something. Do you not think that the analysts would find it more useful if, for example, we told them that the underlying investment was not quite as good as everybody thought that it was? (ASB 1995x, p. 84)

In reply, Paul Davies rightly argued:

> If we are going to give an economic meaning to a balance sheet, we would have to recognise internally-generated assets [because] ... we are ignoring a huge economic meaning in accounts and concentrating on one very narrow issue. If we are to give any economic meaning to accounts, that is the big topic.

The 'narrow issue' in this case, though not explicitly stated, is the apparent wish of Sir David Tweedie to portray a picture of economic reality that remains within the existing transactions or events framework for the recognition of an asset. Within this framework, transactions, directly or indirectly through a RAMV, provide for reliability of measurement, a requirement that is paramount in the recognition process one suspects from Mr Tweedie's viewpoint. So, for example, about internally generated intangibles he says:

> 'How do I value these things? I know that we have been told twice today how we value them, but at least someone wrote a cheque for these. Why do we not just try to get that right first and then move on to the other ones when we get smarter?' (ASB 1995x, p. 85)

In this sense, Paul Davies is quite correct in asserting that we are ignoring a huge economic meaning in the accounts, in this case, for the sake of reliability of measurement offered by transactions, rather than a valuations approach to accounting, certainly at the initial recognition stage of an asset. That does not mean to say that the Davies brothers would support a full-blown valuation-based approach to accounting, far from it; it simply means that Mr Tweedie cannot assert that he is pursuing 'economic meaning' other than in a very selective sense.

According to Will Baxter, an obvious way in which to make sense of goodwill is to say:

> Have accountants perhaps forgotten an asset? ... There is a perfectly respectable asset, we have written it off or the farmer has had some lambs born or something of that sort. This is reasonable. It may be that, in fact, there is an asset. When you say that then you come up against the problem of defining what an asset is. We say that it is the source of future economic benefits and the enterprise has control of it. Then we hastily add 'and it must be measurable'. Although this is not much stressed in the definitions, I think that one ought to say that it could be cut off and transferred to someone else by sale or by gift. It is a marketable unit. I suppose that it follows also that, if it is given away like that and transferred, then what is left is also a viable concern. It is a matter of can you separate Siamese twins, killing one of them? On that definition, some things like patents and so on seem to pass the test. ... As long as criteria are stringent enough, I think that it is wholly beneficial. When you come to brand names, I am afraid that I begin to get very uneasy. Is this really something that Coca Cola could part with and still be a going concern? Can it really be managed satisfactorily? I know that there are eminently respectable institutions that now for a suitable fee will give an impressive valuation, but I hope I am not being indelicate or unkind if I say they remind me somewhat of the tailors who wove the Emperor's new clothes. (ASB 1995x, p. 59)

I shall return to this point later on. David Damant urges the ASB to address the issue of goodwill in the Statement of Principles (ASB 1995z, p. 135); that is, within a conceptual framework in which fundamental issues, such as whether the balance sheet should portray the current value of a company, can be considered. These issues are apparently *a priori* to any consideration of accounting methods, whether that was for goodwill or any other item appearing in the accounts. Mr Hinton replied:

> Well, let us dwell on the conceptual approach. To pursue that we would need to ask ourselves two primary questions, namely, what is the nature of goodwill, what are its characteristics? [question one] Then we would have to ask what are the legitimate needs of users in respect of that goodwill and then we might come up with an ideal solution ... [question two]. (ASB 1995z, p. 136)

One is tempted at this stage to say, exactly, so why was this not the approach of the ASB from the outset? Mr Hinton finishes, '... and then we would have to ask the question can we actually get them relative to reliable information on that basis?' (question three). Almost as an after-thought, we have here an insight from Mr Hinton into the importance of 'reliable information', specifically I would argue, reliability of measurement. The comparison with Will Baxter's earlier comment on the recognition of goodwill as an asset is worth making. Professor Baxter commented:

> We say that it [goodwill] is a source of future economic benefits and the enterprise has control of it [two essential characteristics of an asset]. Then we hastily add 'and it must be measurable' [another characteristic?]. Although this is not much stressed in the definitions [of an asset].

Likewise, it is suggested that Mr Hinton also hastily adds a third question to his 'two primary questions'—the requirement for reliability of measurement, which he articulates in terms of 'reliable information'. Assuming the reader accepts the interpretation of reliability of measurement as the principal requirement for reliable information, the implication here is that it dominates in the asset recognition process. The ASB could have gone down the route of determining asset characteristics for intangibles but it would still have left the thorny issue of their reliable measurement. Though speculative, one suspects that in all probability it would have caused the ASB to consider a full valuations approach to accounting at the initial recognition stage of an asset, something that it was apparently not prepared to do. Let us now contrast a transaction-based cost approach to intangibles with a full valuation-based approach in the next chapter of this book. We are looking at principles here not methods.

9

Consultation, not consensus?

The examination of the public hearing documents is continued here on the two issues that were critical to the earlier part of this book. For example, if you recall, I regarded separability as a critical element in the recognition process affecting intangible assets. I am not alone in this regard. But first, let us consider the desire of the profession to stay within the existing asset recognition boundary created by the requirement for an asset to be recognised on the basis of a recognisable transaction or event.

THE LINKAGE TO THE STATEMENT OF PRINCIPLES

Sir David Tweedie (ASB 1995x, p. 65) noted

> that the responses from academics, bar one or two, have gone for the traditional matching approach, in the sense that they are going to match the purchased goodwill against the future benefits, as they deem it, that have come forward. Presumably, you [Will Baxter] did not teach them this at LSE, so where have they gone wrong?

Will Baxter humorously replied that

> they have not had the benefit of an LSE education if they think that. I am, perhaps unjustifiably, very sceptical of any system that uses the word 'matching'. It seems to me very much to favour not looking at what is going on in the real world, but to look at transfers in a book. If the academics in general come to a particular reason because of a matching argument, I would say that they have gone off the lines. I certainly would want to have a very much fuller explanation from them of why they think that this corresponds to what is happening in the real world as distinct from the figures that a clever accountant can transfer from one account to another.

In contrast, Professor Myddleton said:

> I think there is a danger that the Board all through its activities is mixing up values and costs. Again, you do not have to agree with this, but I think that this is a recognised position that a number of commentators have had. I am an advocate of historical cost accounting. I am not an advocate of mucking around with current values all the time. I appreciate that inevitably that there is some mixture, but I think from the way in which the Board's statement on valuation went earlier, it seems to me that there is a real muddle—maybe there are two schools of thought on the Board itself—and that is from where the difficulty is coming, because, as you well know, unless you agree on from where you are starting or the basic framework of what you are trying to do, you are probably not going to get agreement on what should actually go into the accounts. (ASB 1995y, p. 62)

Allister Wilson also feels 'these questions are vital when considering an issue such as accounting for goodwill. That is something which is quite fundamental not only to this project but also to a number of the ASB's projects' (ASB 1995z, p. 110).

One's approach to goodwill rests fundamentally on whether one has a transactions/matching only view of accounting, favouring historic cost, or a valuation view of accounting, favouring the measurement of internally generated as well as purchased intangibles. Alternatively, there is the current hybrid approach of the above two viewpoints where initial recognition is based on a transaction-based cost with selective remeasurements based on valuations allowed thereafter. In response to Allister Wilson, Sir David Tweedie said:

> You are quite right when you said that it depends where you come from. As Ken [Wild] was saying, we are not terribly interested in internally generated goodwill, just purchased goodwill. We are seeing it as a consolidation difference and going back to the value of the subsidiary. If you look at it in that light and given there are only three things to do—I am thinking of a case in the late 80's which I will not mention, but there is a company that bought its subsidiary for £500 million, say £300 million goodwill, writes it off to reserves in the UK accounts (pre FRS10). Four years later it sells that subsidiary for £220 million and in the absence of UITF3 made a profit of £20 million, when in fact it made a loss of £280 million. Now, no signal was there in the British accounts that something was going on with investment. ... This led us, in effect, to the fact that you could actually give a signal to an analyst that something was going wrong and that is what led us into the impairment test. ... Now what I am concerned about actually is not so much stewardship as information and signals. (ASB 1995z, p. 123)

Mr Tweedie's comments were supported by Mr Wild:

> Chris [Higson] says that there is no information or value in arbitrary write-off or arbitrary amortisation. We are trying to achieve information, genuine information in terms of has the value gone from when you bought—not hair shirt stuff, you know, has the particular business gone, but has the whole value gone. What is the harm in trying to give useful information? (ASB 1995z, p. 122)

Mr Wilson responded, 'The answer is that you are deluding the user into thinking that that goodwill has not been lost or is not dissipated. The answer is it has.' In other words, the asset, if it was one in the first place, has been expensed. Mr Wild's reply was interesting because it highlighted the thought processes behind the distinction between goodwill as an asset and goodwill as an investment, the distinction as far as I am concerned being somewhat tenuous at times. He retorted:

> I did not ask you about goodwill, I asked you about the value inherent in what you are purchasing [which includes goodwill]. What is the problem in giving information about the investment that has been made and its usefulness to the company, where is the harm in that?

To use Sir David Tweedie's example above, capitalise the £300 million goodwill because the company has 'invested' in it, real money has been paid for it and it is a significant 'investment' worth signalling to investors. Such reasoning, it is suggested, attempts to detach itself from the simple logic of whether one is dealing with an asset or an expense. Logically, an investment is an asset and therefore capitalisation is wholly consistent with that viewpoint. Mr Wilson's argument is that the asset or the investment, whichever terminology is preferred, has been lost or dissipated. It has effectively been expensed because a goodwill debit can only be either an asset or an expense and it is not regarded as an asset. It follows, if correct, that capitalisation is wholly inappropriate under these circumstances. It also follows, if correct, that impairment is wholly inappropriate because, if it is an expense, there is nothing to impair. One may have paid a lot of money for it but to capitalise it under such circumstances is akin to capitalising the emperor's new clothes. That was the point being made and it was a fundamental conceptual point to make about the 'assetness' of purchased goodwill.

There were respondents, such as Professor Grinyer and the Davies brothers, who favoured a transaction-based matching approach to accounting for the sake of accurately recording on that well-established and reliable basis in the full understanding that it would not capture the 'full' picture of business reality. David Thompson said:

> You need consistency in the way that these things are valued over time, and you do not want to build in the vagaries of the market place. After all, as I said earlier the balance sheet is not a place to include valuations, in my view. (ASB 1995z, p. 106)

At the heart of the debate here is whether one accepts the relevancy argument or the reliability argument. David Evans said:

> I am noting here what I consider to be the principal objections to the ASB proposal. I believe that it is conceptually flawed. It adopts in part a matching process over the valuation process. Secondly, the issue of principle does not allow for a consensus driven approach. To me a consensus-driven approach is the lowest common denominator accounting, LCD accounting or, perhaps it should be LSD accounting because it has a hallucinatory effect that you have something meaningful. I am afraid that this proposal as it stands to the wider investor public will mean that we do not have something meaningful or understandable. (ASB 1995x, p. 90)

Yet on the first point that the matching concept dominates, according to Mr Cook, Sir David Tweedie does not believe in either the matching concept or the prudence concept (ASB 1995y, p. 67). This surprising revelation is difficult to reconcile with a traditional transaction-based, matching-based approach to accounting, which the ASB still adheres to in most of its pronouncements, for example SSAP2 (ASC 1971). As David Evans indicates, this is in contrast to a valuation-based approach, which is not necessarily reliant on the matching concept and, some may also say, it is an imprudent measurement basis to adopt as a suitable alternative to cost. One suspects, therefore, that this third-party comment may have been expressed in an unguarded moment between colleagues. Yet, we now know with the benefit of hindsight that 'prudence' was subsequently removed from FRS18 on accounting policies (ASB 2001) as an explicit policy (though still implicit to the issue of 'reliability').

According to Professor Michael Page:

> Prudence is an important part of accountability and we can think of prudence as a downward bias in measuring uncertain future amounts. The reason why this is desirable is that it provides a counterweight to the potential that exists in enterprises for excess risk taking whereby equity shareholders can gain wealth transfers from the owners of fixed claims. It seems to me that goodwill of an indefinite life is not prudent. I cannot think of any cases where goodwill could be considered to have an indefinite life and I can think of several converse cases where, apparently, stable businesses with long-term goodwill found that goodwill unexpectedly devalued. The names Perrier and Ratners come to mind. (ASB 1995y, p. 85)

Sir David Tweedie addressed this comment in the following terms:

> Michael, you have mentioned that you believe very firmly in prudence. The ultimate in prudence would be to write goodwill off through the P&L in the first year. Why would you not do that? (ASB 1995y, p. 89)

His reply may be summarised as follows: in principle, one could provide a desirable level of prudence which would have the effect of making management optimally accountable. The world is not like that, but we can have procedures and processes that we know more often work in the real world for assessing what is a desirable level of prudence.

Paul Heaven, managing director of a software development company, offers the following comment on the transaction-based and valuation-based approaches to accounting, which he refers to as two different units of measure:

> This standard deals with the fair value of an asset acquired, whereas the issue relating to [software] development costs is what it suggests, and that is whether or not we put costs on the balance sheet. As I am sure you are all aware, a fair value of an asset may be more than or less than its cost. I would hate to have to try to explain—in what is already a difficult and complex industry—to analysts in the City what the respective differences were in those units of measure. ... The fast moving technological nature of our business means that the fair value is likely to waver by what could be considered to be fairly material amounts. In what is a relatively small sector today, albeit growing rapidly in UK plc, it could do nothing for their confidence in the City and in the institutions constantly to be called upon to explain why such a material asset is wavering in the balance sheet. (ASB 1995y, pp. 16–17)

Clearly, a major issue for ASB concerns the use of valuations on whatever basis. It is that a similar intangible in three different companies could be measured in three different ways (ASB 1995x, p. 54). Thus, reliability of measurement is not assured and comparability suffers as a consequence. It is a point that Weston Anson acknowledged was correct in respect of brand valuations (ASB 1995x, p. 54). In response, Sir David Tweedie said:

> That is a major problem for us then, because one of the things that we have said in the *Statement of Principles* is that, even though we recognise that a brand is an asset, we should not recognise it in the accounts unless it can be measured reliably. The broad definition that we make for that is to say that three or four people will get roughly the same sort of answer. You [Weston Anson] have just scared me by saying that you will get three different answers.

In reply Weston Anson said:

> No, I said three different methods could be used. You might not get three different answers. We might choose to use the replacement method, another client might choose to use the market-based/royalty rate method and another one might choose to use excess cash flow. Theoretically, if we all work accurately, you should get the same answer.

A similar exchange occurred between Mr Cook and Andrew Caldwell of Corporate Valuations (ASB 1995x, p. 10). Some interesting observations flow from this exchange with Mr Anson. Firstly, brands are assets if only because Sir David Tweedie says so, above. Secondly, brand valuations are apparently too subjective for inclusion on the balance sheet. However, reliability of measurement is a subjective concept depending, in part, on who is doing it. Thus, even building values may be subject to wild fluctuations; remember the Queens Moat Properties hotel valuation debacle in 1992. The real challenge is whether it is possible to reduce the subjectivity to an acceptable level by regulating brand accounting practice. For example, in response to Paul Stobart, Mr Hinton said:

> You alluded to the [valuation] methodology becoming more codified. I think that that is probably a fair comment. In fact, the methodologies have codified over the last five, six years or so, but there are still a number of methods. He asked: Do you see a situation developing, as we have in the surveyors' property appraisal field, where the methods will not only be codified, but actually the appropriate methodology in each accepted circumstance will be promulgated. So that readers could actually be assured that we would be using common methodology for given circumstances to avoid a situation where we are going to have three brand valuations or even more on a given asset? (ASB 1995y, p. 30)

The short answer was yes, but to date no such codification exists. Sir David Tweedie asked Weston Anson whether there was any evidence for reliability of measurement in the valuation methods used by his company. He asked 'if there was any evidence that these methods are borne out by ultimate sales or something like that' (ASB 1995x, p. 54). In reply, Mr Anson said:

> In fact, we track that kind of information and, typically, replacement cost or conversion cost tends to be the floor value and sales of intangibles (whether it is a brand name or a piece of technology) will tend to be slightly higher than replacement value or conversion values. Market values, on the other hand, tend to be pretty good predictors. Again speaking from experience, we do a fair amount of valuation for clients who are about either to sell or acquire an asset. We find that by using the inputted royalty rate or marked-based valuation method, we can come within plus or minus 10 per cent always and often times closer to that. It is not an exact science, but neither is real estate appraisal. It is still open to interpretation.

From Mr Anson's reply it is not clear whether the valuation, plus or minus 10%, is subsequently proven by the transaction-based amount for its purchase or sale but one assumes that is the case. If so, then prima facie this would be impressive empirical evidence of the reliability of his valuations. However, one also needs to be careful about circularity here in that the valuation may actually be determining the price such that the subsequent transaction-based amount and the valuation validate each other in a mutually reinforcing manner.

Professor Whittington cast doubt on the accuracy of valuation-based approaches in the measurement of intangibles by asking, 'Can you audit them and will the rest of the world recognise it as good information? I am really asking you [Anthony Morton] whether there is some objective test' (ASB 1995x, p. 72). In referring to the portfolio of his company's newspaper titles, Mr Morton said:

> We take an expected cash flow for those and convert that into a net present value. You can do that and you get something that is pretty close to what is a market value for those businesses. It is getting closer to goodwill, I will admit that.

It would appear from this response that Mr Morton believes his company can provide 'good information' through the use of net present values that approximate to market values. However, one suspects that a readily ascertainable market value for newspaper titles does not exist and therefore the assertion is difficult to substantiate. According to Graham Swetman, the approach of the public hearings rely upon an ill-conceived reappraisal of the purpose of the balance sheet. At present the balance sheet really contains amounts that are all capable of reasonably precise measurement, give or take a little on the property side. It does not pretend to be a valuation of the business which can only be determined really by market forces. The difference between book and market values represents the goodwill associated with business, whether it is purchased or internally generated. This will, therefore, include a whole variety of intangibles, including brands, technology, dealer networks, market positions and the management teams. If you are going to include very arbitrary valuations for some of these items why not include measures for them all? (ASB 1995x, p. 37)

He argues that the present system allows a reasonable degree of comparability and that the ASB's proposals would lead to considerable confusion to the non-expert user. However, it has to be said that there are those who would offer the opposite approach; for example, that balance sheets which already present multiple measurement bases are de facto lacking in comparability. Also the non-expert user is probably already confused, for example, by the accounting distinction between capitalised purchased intangibles and those uncapitalised internally generated intangibles. From their viewpoint, an intangible asset exists and creates wealth, or it does not. The distinction between purchased or non-purchased intangibles, one could argue, is irrelevant to them.

Even if one adopts the consistency of measurement associated with a mainstream transaction-based view of accounting, the regulatory framework may nevertheless allow for variations in accounting practice and therefore inconsistency in disclosure. Consider the comments of Paul Heaven on the capitalisation of software:

> The computer software and services industry does not appear to be able to make up its mind about whether or not it should hold in the balance sheet the value of its computer software. It could be seen as deferred expenditure under SSAP22 [now replaced by FRS10] or under development under SSAP13. It would be permitted, and indeed some companies do, to treat the development costs of their software as expenditure of a capital nature. (ASB 1995y, p. 14)

So, for those who would advance the case for reliability of measurement afforded by a purely transaction-based view of accounting, the multiplicity of allowable accounting treatments reduces such reliability at least for comparative purposes. It was also interesting to note that, according to Mr Heaven, 'only six, today, out of sixty public-quoted software and services companies have any material form of intangible asset on their balance sheet' (ASB 1995y, p. 14). The most common accounting treatment, which requires no SSAP/FRS, is simply to expense software immediately through the profit and loss (P&L) account (ASB 1995y, p. 16). However, there was concern that, whilst the write-off approach was consistent with the accounting treatment of internally generated software, there were situations where the use of alternative accounting methods may be guided by the need to disclose a reasonable profit, particularly post acquisition. He said:

> Let me promise you that the make-in or buy-out decision made for 'Kalamazoo Answer' would be fundamentally different had we been faced with the prospect of writing off £6 million to our profit and loss account and the headline reported figures of the group in the year in which we acquired that. Certainly, in the case of the mega-takeover in our industry recently by Misys of ACT, that would have wiped out their profits, for now and some years to come, off the operating line. (ASB 1995y, p. 17)

Paul Heaven referred to the difference between purchased and internally generated software as

> no more than a make-in or buy-out type decision. ... Furthermore, it to me makes no sense, because the value shown in the balance sheet clearly does not represent the total value of the intellectual property rights of the software products that we as a group own. Indeed, it therefore follows that the amortisation charge does not reflect the total cost of depreciation, if you like, of the assets we own. I repeat that it makes the accounts difficult to interpret and, I would argue, even misleading. (ASB 1995y, p. 16)

Mr Heaven rejected the ASB's accounting choices in the discussion and working papers in favour of what he referred to as a big bang charge to the P&L account. The consequences for the bottom line are obvious but entirely consistent with a view that some, or all, of the premium paid to acquire a business is not an asset by nature. Andrew Caldwell put forward the case that

> there are strong arguments for valuing what might be described as internally-generated intellectual property rights. ... I see no fundamental reason, as a layman, why the future income streams applicable to that intellectual property cannot be capitalised in a similar way to those which have been acquired. In that regard, I think that we would go beyond the Board's proposal that there should just be a ready market in respect of such intangibles. ... We would go on to propose that internally generated intellectual property or intangible assets, which fulfil the criteria that have been suggested for intellectual property on acquisition, should be valued. (ASB 1995x, p. 8)

Those criteria, however, are difficult to discern from Mr Caldwell's response but they appear to be the attachment of legal rights, an identifiable life and the existence of an income stream from the intangible asset (ASB 1995x, p. 7). In response to Mr Caldwell, Mr Cook asked him a very searching, yet simple, question: 'Could you tell us whether there is any difference in the way in which you would set about valuing the future cash flows of a company and valuing the future cash flows of the intangible assets?' (ASB 1995x, p. 10). The reply may be summarised as follows: there are different valuation techniques for the valuation of different assets. This is not very satisfactory because such variation does not necessarily assist in the search for 'sufficient reliability' in the measurement of worth. One suspects that Mr Cook was intimating that there is no difference and that therefore the identification of income streams attributable to intangibles for valuation purposes is confused with income streams as a whole. Also that the separation of the two is problematic.

Sir David Tweedie pursued Mr Caldwell on the idea of capitalising internally generated intangibles independently of a known transaction-based cost:

> At least if you purchase something, whether it is goodwill or brands, there is a ceiling: you have written a cheque or you have issued shares that you can value and so on. How confident do you feel that the values that you are getting are actually realistic? Have there been any sales of these intangibles that you can verify or is there any evidence that we can see to show that these things are useful? (ASB 1995x, p. 13)

To the apparent dissatisfaction of the chairman, the response of Mr Caldwell was to advance the merits of valuations without necessarily being able to refer to an established market as a benchmark, as with for example the Royal Institute of Chartered Surveyors (RICS) indices on movements in property values. Nevertheless, Mr Caldwell stated:

> There is a market for intellectual property: A more common way of going forward is
> by licensing. . . . There is an awful lot more information about licensing of intellectual
> property.

It would appear that Sir David Tweedie remained unconvinced, because he then addressed
the valuation methods themselves, in particular the use of net present values, citing David
Damant's objections to the use of future profits for valuation purposes.

The exchange between Sir David Tweedie and Mr Caldwell was interesting because
Mr Tweedie, it is suggested, sought to undermine the current approaches to valuations as
unreliable, which is not a hard thing to do. However, Mr Caldwell touched on a pertinent
point when he stated:

> It is rather like the chicken and the egg if there is no standard accounting policy upon
> the treatment of intangible assets or no perceived one, and that to some extent is why
> we are here today. I think that once the guidelines are laid down on the valuation
> of intangible assets, then one can build up this bank of information. It is relatively
> patchy at the moment because not everyone goes through that process. What I would
> say is that it is being refined. (ASB 1995x, p. 14)

The comment was interesting because Mr Caldwell effectively placed the onus on the
ASB to rise to the challenge of reducing the subjectivity of valuations by regulating an
approach to them that would gain acceptability by the subsequent widespread adoption
of that technique. Hence the chicken and egg argument in that regulation establishes
conformity, which hopefully establishes consistency, which is self-reinforcing because
everyone relies on it for financial information purposes, but first there must be reliability
of measurement. The point here was that the ASB was apparently not up to that particular
challenge, preferring instead to rely on the existing recognition boundary of a known
transaction-based cost or a transaction-based RAMV. This approach could be likened to
an ostrich burying its head in the sand.

Kevin Plummer, on the other hand, believed that

> transactions for brands are clearly possible in theory and have occurred on a very
> limited number of occasions that [it] would establish the principle for the type of asset.
> Thereafter, I think it should be a question of judgement as to whether management
> and auditors believe the criteria established to have been met. (ASB 1995z, p. 22)

This would be an interesting development in that asset recognition has always been on
the basis of a known transaction for a specific asset. Yet asset recognition post FRS10
can now be on the basis of a RAMV, as evidenced by a market of frequent transactions
for a similar, not a specific, transacted asset. Mr Plummer's suggestion would relax the
recognition criteria still further in that transactions 'on a very limited number of occasions'
might be sufficient for asset recognition purposes.

Sir David Tweedie, in respect of intangibles, argued that 'one of the problems with
which we are faced is how do we separate between something that is fairly similar to
goodwill but is not quite goodwill? What is the difference?' (ASB 1995y, p. 79). He asked
Mark Armour and Alex Minford of Reed Elsevier (UK) Ltd, 'You have 500 million of
intangible assets, some goodwill and some publishing titles, how do you split them?' Sir
David argued that other intangibles are similar to goodwill, however, purchased goodwill
is operationally defined as a 'difference', as per SSAP22/FRS10. Being pedantic, one
could easily argue that what he is actually asking is, What is the difference between

a defined 'difference' and other intangibles? The questioning is measurement focused without recognition of the substance (assuming there is any) of what has been disclosed. Likewise, the reply was measurement focused:

> It is a question of valuation and, clearly, we can identify the intangible asset. What we attempt to do is to place what we think is a fair, but conservative value on that asset. I think, as the discussion points out, or maybe it is in some of the responses, with intangible assets and in many other areas, any number of valuers can come up with different valuations, but what we attempt to do is to place the valuation that is sensible. A methodology that is consistently applied can be monitored. We then look to see whether there are any changes that might suggest that we have actually been getting it wrong. So far we have found that the method that we have applied has been a consistent basis for attributing value.

Sir David Tweedie sought to establish some empirical support for this last assertion so he asked, when Reed Elsevier sold some of its titles, whether they had any gains or losses on the sales compared to book value. Mark Armour provided an interesting though inherently limited insight into the reliability of valuations:

> We have had a number of gains and we have had some losses, once the goodwill is brought back under UITF3. It is not significant amounts, I am happy to say, but certainly we are able to attribute the relevant intangible asset value to the title being disposed of with quite some ease. (ASB 1995y, p. 79)

Mr Armour acknowledged the subjectivity of the valuations, indicating that if two valuers arrived at the same value, it would probably be due to luck rather than judgement:

> One publishing group may have a different outlook on a particular publishing asset from another—that might have things to do with market leadership, market share and critical mass in a particular sector—so there will be variations in value. I repeat that for what we are looking is something that could be relied upon in a consistent manner. (ASB 1995y, p. 80)

Perhaps this is the 'trade-off' that the ASB should be looking for in the field of intangible asset measurement: 'consistency' for 'reliability' based on an ex-post rationalisation of the variation between book value and market values within 'acceptable' levels of tolerance.

In his introductory comments, Neil Chisman comments on the usefulness of a balance sheet that excludes many intangible assets:

> I believe that the lay user of accounts broadly expects the balance sheet to reflect some concept of what the business is worth. He expects the totals to represent values with a lay concept. The current treatment of both goodwill and intangibles is a major impediment to those user expectations. Unless we get a closer reflection of the layman's concept of value into the balance sheet, I think, as David has said many times, the British balance sheet will then be destined to be meaningless. It will just simply be adding apples to oranges and hoping that the total means something to somebody. (ASB 1995x, pp. 17–18)

The appeal of Mr Chisman to user expectations is a common strategy of those seeking to change the content of the balance sheet. Similarly, the reference to values with a lay concept and the adding of apples to oranges, is a common strategy of those seeking a change to the basis of measurement. In the first instance, the appeal is directed towards 'relevancy' as evidenced by the inclusion of internally generated intangibles on the balance sheet. In the second instance, the appeal one suspects is directed towards the use of a single measurement method, rather than the present multiple basis, based on a layman's view of value.

Most of the questions fielded against Mr Chisman were directed at these two positions. In the case of the first point about 'relevancy', Mr Chisman, it is argued, effectively points to the restrictive nature of the existing transactions or events asset recognition boundary. He does so by reference to the following example of an intangible asset that is initially outside it and then subsequently captured within it after being sold. He asks us to consider

> a business that has been built up by advertising starting from scratch, such that it has very few tangible assets [let us say none], but it makes a profit of £1 million a year, largely from the intangible assets of a customer list and reputation. If this business is then sold for £10 million, consider the balance sheet before and after the sale. Before the sale, there are no assets in the balance sheet, after the sale there is goodwill of £10 million in the balance sheet of the acquiring company, but, of course, the business has not changed. Clearly, before the sale there was an intangible with a value of £10 million and we should work to allow that intangible to be recognised in order to bring meaning to the balance sheet. (ASB 1995x, p. 19)

Mr Chisman comments that he 'does not think that it is reasonable that the accounting standard should allow the same economic entity to be validly accounted for with two completely different balance sheets.' I would also draw the reader's attention again to Mirror Group and Trinity Mirror (Chapter 5) for an example of such anomalies.

With regard to the second position, the layman's view of value is often expressed in terms of the present value of future cash flows. However, the subjectivity of such an approach is well documented. Professor Whittington had an interesting comment to make about how the ASB had its knuckles rapped by the constituency when it attempted to include forecasting, presumably inclusive of the present value of cash flows, in the operating and financial review statement of published annual accounts:

> I will read to you a telling sentence from another submission to us by somebody who is going to appear this afternoon. It says, 'those who are familiar with the use of present values in the preparation of capital expenditure proposals will attest to the ease with which these calculations can be made to support a case.' I must say, although I understand the theoretical attractions of forecasting, that does ring rather true. Do you not think that there is a basis for financial reporting? If forecasting is still some way away and, therefore, even the application of ceiling tests to goodwill that has a measurable transaction behind it is quite adventurous, are we not going far enough at the moment? (ASB 1995x, p. 25)

In response, Mr Chisman argued that in fudging cash flows the directors would be storing up future problems because 'there is going to come a time when you can no longer forecast those cash flows going into the future and something is going to plummet. Concepts of prudence and auditability and so on will start to take over' (ASB 1995x, p. 26).

The more interesting aspect is that Professor Whittington states that the ASB is going 'far enough at the moment'. Indeed, the subsequent FRS11 on the impairment of fixed assets (ASB 1998) is adventurous in that it includes discounted cash flow (DCF) techniques in a substantive and formalised manner for what I believe is the first time in current financial regulations. It represents the inclusion of one more measurement basis in an accounting system already based on the use of multiple measurement bases. In the case of DCF approaches, however, Professor Whittington's assertion that the ceiling tests applicable to goodwill have a measurable transaction behind them is perhaps stretching the linkage of DCF values to transaction-based costs too far: DCF is future based whereas transaction-based cost is usually historical.

Contrast this situation with the case of RAMVs. The attachment of a RAMV to a measurable transaction is evidenced by frequent transactions in an established market. Not so with DCF approaches which present a degree of crystal ball gazing based on 'up-to-date budgets and plans' rather than evidence of frequent transactions (ASB 1998, p. 23). Professor Whittington's comment is interesting because it appears to show not only a long-term desire to move to a measurement system based entirely on economic values, which would probably satisfy the layman as well, but also a reluctance to move away from the initial recognition of an asset on any basis other than a known transaction-based cost. Some authors have likened this stance to holding tight to nanny's hand for fear of something worse.

With a RAMV, the evidence of frequent transactions is taken from a homogeneous population. Weston Anson, however, argues that

> we all know that in the business world there is no such thing as an exact comparable or identical asset. It simply does not exist. However, what does exist usually is a larger group of similar assets. Let us say that you have an internally-generated brand or an internally generated technology that is unique. You can find in the universe a range of similar intangible assets to which it can be compared and from which you can predicate its value. (ASB 1995x, p. 50)

Of course, such an approach assumes that the comparison is a valid one and that a value is correctly determined on some differential basis rather than according to an absolute benchmark.

The measurement of value is also somewhat problematic. For example, Weston Anson says, 'We believe that you can set specific market values for all intangible assets and, when you have difficulty finding a market value, then a replacement or a substitution value can be established' (ASB 1995x, p. 50). A counter-argument, however, is that the market value is set by the market and that one of the problems with measuring some intangibles is that the market is, at best, thin and sometimes non-existent. Further, determining replacement values on something that is as unique as, say, the Rolls-Royce brand must involve a high degree of subjectivity. Nevertheless, Weston Anson believes that 'brands are no more unique than any other intangible asset.'

Let us summarise so far. There are two very distinct approaches here: one directed towards a full valuations approach to accounting and the other towards the maintenance of a transaction-based cost approach, most particularly at the initial recognition stage of an asset. At the heart of these approaches, respectively, is the age-old argument between the relevance of the figures produced by accountants and the reliability of the measurement presented thereby. However, I have argued that reliability is a subjective assessment and that the real challenge is to find ways of reducing this subjectivity. One way is to retreat to a traditional transactions/matching approach to accounting because, without doubt, it is a tried and tested approach and within its well-known limitations it has proved itself to be both robust and reliable. However, this does not fit well with an agenda that seeks to portray economic meaning, which favours the use of current values and related valuation methods. From what I can see, this appears to be the intention of the ASB, but I also observe a deep reluctance to move away from a transaction-based cost approach, certainly at the initial recognition stage of an asset.

It seems to me that the ASB is stuck in no-man's-land between the two approaches and it really needs to make up its mind which approach should dominate. I have argued for a full valuations approach because I believe the issue of relevancy is now far stronger than the issue of reliability. Were it not for regulatory compliance, Companies Act and taxation, I believe the profession could die, and rightly so, because the information we now portray on the balance sheet, I would suggest, in most cases, is fairly useless to the users of them. The profession has no automatic right to survival and it is lucky in occupying what is virtually a monopolistic position in certain fields of financial regulation. But there is no doubt that the dominance the profession enjoys is under attack by many outside the profession, for example brand valuers, who play the relevance card to the full and in the process undermine the position of the accounting profession. It must either rise to the 'subjectivity challenge' posed by a valuations approach, or perhaps not die, but certainly become less relevant to the business community in terms of what is used by them for decision-making purposes.

Let us now address the issue of separability, which also has two distinct approaches. One of them, I have already argued, is inextricably linked to transaction-based measurements.

THE ROLE OF SEPARABILITY

The issue of separability can be approached from two different perspectives. The measurement perspective is based on the idea that if the intangible can be measured reliably as, for example, with the transaction-based cost of purchased goodwill, then the accurate determination of a value, in this case at cost, simultaneously establishes its separable identity as an intangible asset. In this context, Mr Cook asked Mr Caldwell whether he saw intangible assets as more separable than goodwill because they were valued on an external basis, for example using relevant market data, rather than on an internal basis (ASB 1995x, p. 11). It is interesting that Mr Caldwell's response adopted the second alternative perspective on separability—irrespective of an asset's value, it is, or it is not, individually separable from the other assets of a business. In other words, an asset is separable by nature independently of its worth. Indeed, it is logically prior to any consideration of worth. On this point he argues that the question you have to decide is, 'Can they operate separately and still have a value? I think that if the answer is no they cannot, then you should not give them individual values' (ASB 1995x, p. 12). This was a firm stance to adopt on the separable nature of assets, which it is suggested was then undermined by the subsequent comment that if they have a 'combined value, then it should be done on that basis.' In other words, a collection of assets, including intangibles, will suffice for valuation purposes but this does not establish their separable identity other than for combined measurement purposes. Archer, on the other hand, is quite clear 'that measurability per se is not a recognition criteria nor should it be one. First of all, you have to decide whether the object is an asset, whether it meets the recognition criteria for an asset, and then you move to the question of measurability' (ASB 1995y, p. 69).

Mr Caldwell's response is consistent with an overall view of separability on a spectrum. That is, a spectrum with, at one end, 'hard' intangibles like patents which are clearly separable by nature and, at the other end, 'soft' intangibles like customer lists with an inseparable nature but which nevertheless might be valued as a combination of assets. In that sense they are separable only as a combination of assets. Assuming one accepts the notion of a spectrum, it is interesting to observe how at the 'hard' end separability takes on the characteristics of the Companies Act definition of it, whilst at the 'soft' end separability takes on the characteristics consistent with a measurement separability view of it. In other words, it is a spectrum that changes its nature from asset recognition at the hard end to asset measurement at the soft end of it. As such, it casts doubts on its consistency and validity as a spectrum at all.

Mr Garner, however, interpreted the notion of a spectrum rather differently. He argued, in respect of brands from fast-moving consumer goods (FMCG) companies like Guinness plc, that

> separability is fairly easy ... but I think equally it would be very difficult for instance for some industrial companies where they have very strong brand names ... Therefore, one is bound to be looking at a spectrum. You [Guinness plc] have your kind of company at one extreme, and you have industrial companies of the kind I have just outlined at the other. Somewhere in the middle of all that there has to be one of these hard dividing lines which either fall one side or the other. (ASB 1995z, p. 21)

The 'hard dividing line' advanced in this work is asset recognition, not measurement, on the basis of recognition of an artefact within a boundary established by the requirement for a legally separable identity. In this regard it would not, for example, depend on the strength of a brand but whether the brand was legally separable and recognisable as an artefact. The artefact in this case would be its related trademark. As such, spectrums become irrelevant—it is legally separable or not.

Mr Wild expressed some reservations about another dual perspective on the issue of separability, namely, that intangible assets are separable individually or in combination or, as Mr Anson expressed it, as bundles (ASB 1995x, p. 55). From Mr Wild's viewpoint the former perspective, individually separable intangibles, was apparently the correct one, so he asked Weston Anson how his bundling concept tied in with his notion of separability. Weston Anson replied:

> First of all when you have major intangibles, they should be valued separately and discretely. The bundling concept is useful for companies who have a whole range of small and medium sized intangibles, no one of which might be worth more than several hundred thousands or perhaps one or two million pounds. Taken together as a bundle, they may make a meaningful bundle of intangibles. It is a useful way to value intangibles when you are trying to conglomerate values for a great number of small and medium-sized ones, but wherever possible do them individually.

It is probably fair to say that the need to create a valuation on whatever separable basis, individually or as bundles, is the driving force here. However, the preference was clearly for separable identification of intangibles on an individual basis (ASB 1995x, p. 56). Will Baxter too, despite asserting that separability should be a feature of the definition of an asset (ASB 1995x, p. 62), also appears to support the measurement of intangibles in bundles (ASB 1995x, p. 63):

> Incidentally, I think that one of the admirable parts of your draft is that it does allow for this phenomenon of jointness. I am not sure, but I would be inclined to bet that the majority of assets have benefits that cannot be measured separately. You can measure the team's benefits but not any one of them.

Mr Cook pursued the idea of the separable identification of intangibles from goodwill:

> Is not one of the problems when you are stripping down the intangibles to value at a lower and lower level that, essentially, you have a whole number of them that are all relying on the same cash flow to justify them? Is there not then a huge problem either of double counting or at the very least allocation? (ASB 1995x, p. 56)

The first thing to note about this comment is that it is entirely measurement focused. Separability is not addressed according to nature but according to whether it can be measured separately and reliably. The comment is not invalid, in fact Mr Anson agreed with it, but the issue of measurement is concurrent with the issue of separable recognition of an intangible asset. However, it is possible to argue that separable recognition of an intangible asset according to whether it is separable by nature is logically prior to measurement as the means of recognition.

When asked a question about the separableness of intangible assets such as brands and newspaper titles, Will Baxter responded:

> I think that you will find that the *Times*, for example, would have great difficulty in meeting the criteria that you lay down. How could the *Times* part with the title the *Times* and still keep its circulation and so on? How could Coca Cola part with its name and still keep going? Would there not be a wholesale disruption of distribution systems, staff and so on that you really cannot think of the name as something distinct from the firm itself? (ASB 1995x, p. 61)

In response, Professor Whittington asked, 'So separability is a key criterion in defining an asset?' Will Baxter replied:

> I should have thought so. You may be able to think of examples where that is not true. I should be interested to hear of them. It seems to me that it is a very good step to defining an asset.

Here separability is according to an asset's nature, what may be called an input viewpoint. The existing definition of an asset, however, is expressed in terms of outputs, that is, what it produces in terms of future economic benefits. To change the definition of an asset to include items such as separability raises important questions about the source or resource from which those future economic benefits are derived. It could, for example, cause one to rethink one's position on the capitalisation of goodwill, as per FRS10. Purchased goodwill is transaction based; it is assumed to produce future economic benefits as per the definition of an asset, but it is certainly not separable from the assets of the business which has been acquired. Finally, there is no doubt that separating the *Times* and Coca-Cola brands from the other assets of their businesses would cause immense disruption and financial loss. However, they are measures of their worth not their separableness which, firstly, are legally separable by virtue of their trademarks and, secondly, they are not impossible to replace, they are simply going to be very expensive to replace. Consider, for example, the replacement of the Andersen Consulting brand with the new Accenture brand—expensive not impossible! However, the view of the inseparable nature of a brand appears to be deeply ingrained in the philosophical perspective of some members of the ASB. For example, Mr Cook said:

> It does seem to me that the separability argument that you [Andy Simmonds] were applying to justify the separability of brands is a difficult one to launch, because

you have to ask 'What is it separable from?' It seems to me that essentially it is
separable from the business that is represented by that brand. So almost by definition
it is not separable. The brand is trying to encapsulate the business and you cannot
do that business if you have lost the brand. May be you can continue to manufacture
something, but it will not be what it was you were formerly selling under that brand.
(ASB 1995z, p. 75)

The key phrase here is that 'you cannot do that business if you have lost the brand'. The
previous example shows that that is not the case. It is simply going to be very expensive
in terms of marketing to re-establish in a different guise what was lost or sold. Perhaps a
more valid argument would be to say that it may be so expensive to replace certain brands
that it is not economically viable. In other words, the financial damage of separating the
brand from the business is outweighed by the income from its sale, but that is a different
argument to saying you cannot do the business. Mr Cook is quite right in saying that in
some cases the remaining business 'will not be what it was' without its related brand. In
some cases it may even be positively beneficial to jettison an unsuccessful brand.

Mr Cook highlighted a practical problem associated with the separability of intangibles
where tangibles and intangibles are sold at the same time. He asked Mr Sugden whether
he was

using the question of whether or not tangible assets would change hands at the same
time as the intangible assets, as a test of separability. Do you think that it always has
to be associated with tangible assets? After all, the Companies Act talks of separability
as being something that can be disposed of without disposing of a business and it does
not necessarily identify a business with tangible assets. (ASB 1995y, p. 12)

Mr Cook's question is important because it implies that intangible assets by nature, rather
than by measurement, are actually inseparable from the tangible assets acquired by a business. Consider purchased goodwill, which is a separable measurement but not separable by
nature from the other assets purchased as part of a business acquisition. The implication is
obvious: if by nature intangibles are generally inseparable from the tangibles on acquisition
of a business then this tends to support the ASB's stance towards the subsumption of intangibles within a purchased goodwill 'difference'. Let us consider Mr Sugden's response:

I think that the trouble is that, if you have got tangibles and intangible assets for
which you paid £10 million, how do you subdivide that, whereas, if, for instance,
the proprietors of the *Times* sold the title, they would just sell the title and it would
get produced and printed by another company? Part of my reason here is that a little
while ago now I was talking to clearing banks and I was asking them, when they
were sizing up how much they should lend to somebody, what notice did they take
of goodwill. And I remember they particularly said that where something can be sold
separately then they would regard that as reasonable security: like a publisher's back
list, even if the publishers then turned bad, his back list can be sold off.

The interesting comparison here is with Will Baxter's comment that the *Times* was inseparable from the other assets of its business—not so according to Alan Sugden.

The problem of separating intangibles from tangibles was also a problem in respect
of the capitalisation of pharmaceutical licences. Such licences are attached to property.
Thus whilst in theory there is no fixed life to a licence, it can in practice be affected
by the life of a property. In contrast, many hotel groups regard their hotel properties
as having an indefinite life because they are constantly maintained to a high standard.
Stephen Sampson said that in a business acquisition,

> separating the premises [chemist shops] is relatively easy as there are well developed
> valuation procedures in this area which are independent of the use of the premises.
> However, remaining value, the bulk remains to the holding of the retail pharmacy
> licence and the protection this gives to the income stream of the business. It is not
> possible to separate this easily from purchased goodwill of which there must be some,
> as it relates to the acquisition costs of a profitable business. In this situation where
> separation is difficult it is obvious that the bulk of the amount relates to an intangible
> asset rather than purchased goodwill. It would be very useful if the whole amount
> could be attributed to the intangible asset. (ASB 1995z, p. 27)

Of course, if it was wholly attributable to the purchased licences then it may well hide the
possibility that some of the goodwill may, in some circumstances, constitute an overpayment to acquire the business. Also, the implication here is that goodwill is viewed in what
may be regarded as its traditional, abstract sense as business reputation, good customer
relations, and so on. This tends to attach to the premises and the people who conduct
business in them rather than to pharmaceutical licences. It follows that if a licence was
transferred to another premises or proprietor then the goodwill, in the above traditional
sense, may well die and be worth nothing. The bottom line is that goodwill is inseparable
from the other assets of a business, whether they be the pharmaceutical licence, proprietor
or premises, and therefore there is considerable doubt about its status as an asset in the
first place.

In respect of brands and trademarks, Paul Stobart says they are legally separable and
'we are delighted to see that there is an overwhelming majority in favour of that' (ASB
1995y, p. 28). But Professor Whittington remained unconvinced:

> You have defined it as a legal right, but, of course, there is not a legal instrument called
> a brand actually. There is a bundle of legal rights, I imagine, patents, trademarks and
> copyrights. How do you relate these to define a brand? (ASB 1995y, p. 31)

Paul Stobart responded that he

> defined the brand as a trademark supported by the legal status of a trademark. A brand
> is a trademark that is in use, that is the best way to describe it. A trademark in use
> involves a collection of intangible elements which in their entirety could represent what
> marketing people get very excited about and that is what we are trying to measure.
> There is the name, the graphic design, the logo, the get-up and there is the image of
> reputation, all of which can be packaged and seen discretely as being support for that
> trademark. Indeed, I think that all the moves that are being made in the trademark
> field, in terms of European directives and recent trademark legislation, shows that you
> can trademark a lot more than just the pure name. You can trademark the shape, the
> smell, the colour and the sound of that particular trademark as a base. I think that
> there is a collection of legal rights that represent the brand.

A collection of legal rights, however, does not imply that they only operate as a collection.
Nevertheless, it was a point that Professor Whittington seized on because one suspects it
was a way of undermining the separability of specific intangibles, particularly brands, so
that their subsumption within goodwill became the more plausible option from a regulatory
viewpoint. He asked:

> If I have a licence to manufacture or a licence to distribute, but I do not own the
> original patent or whatever it is, and I have a copyright over the packaging, the three
> together constitute a brand do they?

The learned Professor obviously ignored Mr Stobart's earlier response on the constituent nature of a brand in relation to its trademark. He pressed on:

> When I come to value it then, do I just look at for what I could sell the trademark or do I look at my rights to distribute? After all, the trademark would not be any good: if it is a drug or something and somebody else holds the patent and so on, I would not be able to manufacture and distribute it. I would not be able to do anything with the trademark without the other things.

Mr Stobart said, 'That is not true.' He rightly acknowledged the trademark and patent locked together in some circumstances are a very powerful combination but that the brand could survive long after the patent expired. It is at this juncture that the two views on separability become apparent. Mr Stobart views separability according to a legally separable nature and life (e.g. 15 years for the patent and perhaps indefinitely for the trademarked brand). With respect to Professor Whittington, having lost the separability argument on the basis of a legally separable nature and life, he switched the debate to the alternative tack of measurement separability and the need for reliability of measurement. He pressed the earlier point again but this time from a measurement viewpoint:

> When you are valuing it, do you just take the rent that you can get from the trademark or do you take any excess cash flows that you think will derive from distribution or manufacture?

Mr Stobart responded that

> in terms of separability, there are a lot of very well developed tests to make sure that we are identifying a stream of earnings that is brand related rather than related to any of the other tangible or intangible assets employed by that business. (ASB 1995y, p. 33)

If correct, then one would probably award maximum points to Mr Stobart in this exchange. However, the key issue here in respect of measurement separability is actually reliability of measurement, and on that point Mr Stobart still has a battle on his hands to convince his critics on the validity of the valuation approaches adopted by valuation companies.

Mr Wild sought to distinguish asset recognition prior to asset measurement in the following terms:

> I saw two characteristics in there with the word 'measuring', one characteristic being measurable, and that was a characteristic that we were using to determine when something was recognisable; the second characteristic is the actual measurement itself, which I would agree with you comes out to the recognition. Do you see any merit in that split? (ASB 1995y, p. 75)

This is a classic restatement of the role of measurement separability in the asset recognition process, entirely measurement focused. Logically, if something is measurable then it is capable of measurement and all that remains is to decide whether measurement will take place. Thus, the value of an internally generated intangible asset is measurable but measurement rarely takes place for reporting purposes within the existing accounting framework. The real issue here is the reliability of that measurement which is separate from and logically subsequent to the issue of asset recognition. The distinction between measurable and measurement therefore seems to be somewhat spurious. Archer would probably agree:

I think that it is dangerous. That is why I prefer the word 'separable'. I come back to the point that the business engages in a number of expenditures whose purpose is to create value for the future. In a historical cost context these can be measured on a historical cost basis. One could just add up the debits, so to speak. That within a historical cost context is regarded as a perfectly respectable way of measuring an asset. Once you go down that route, you have the Pandora's box with all kinds of funny things flying out, as we find in French financial reporting: customer lists and you name it. Maybe some of them are genuinely separable, but plenty are not. I would prefer to have the word 'separability' as a recognition criterion, even though it might mean something quite close to what you mean by measurability. I just think that 'measurability' is a bit of a dangerous word to use for that particular purpose. (ASB 1995y, p. 75)

To summarise, the notion of measurement separability proposes asset recognition on the basis of a measurement. Thus, it is also consistent with an asset definition focused on measurable outcomes, that is, future economic benefits. It follows that it is also consistent with the ASB's economic outlook for accounting. I have effectively argued for a return to what Napier and Power (1992) have argued are lingering physicalist and legalist prejudices. There are clearly many ways of interpreting separability. I have chosen the physicalist approach in terms of the requirement for a recognisable artefact for an intangible asset. I have chosen the legalist approach in terms of such recognition being within a boundary created by the requirement for a legally separable identity as per the Companies Act definition of separability. The underpinning logic is simple: recognition before measurement, not recognition on the basis of a measurement. Otherwise, one cannot be too sure what one is measuring. Personally, I think it is for this reason that the goodwill and intangible assets debate will not go away. The profession has a temporary reprieve post FRS10, but in the long term as goodwill dominates the balance sheet, the pressure to explain the nature of this embarrassment will simply grow and grow.

I have addressed the apparent consistency of a measurement separability approach linked to the UK's 'measurement focused' asset definition, linked to an economic outlook for accountancy. But the whole approach is constrained by a legal requirement, mainly a contractual requirement, for asset recognition to be triggered by past transactions or events. So I would argue that the criticism of lingering physicalist and legalist prejudices is inherent in the existing transaction-based approach to accounting. I have also argued that, despite arguments to the contrary, measurement separability actually prejudices a transaction-based approach and therefore predominantly one based on cost. At least with my suggestions the asset recognition boundary is broadened to include many more intangible assets than at present. The measurement method is then not necessarily tied to the asset recognition process and the profession can then embrace a wider perspective on asset measurement at least from a disclosure viewpoint. Let us hope it can rise to the challenge.

Bibliography

Aaker, D. A. (1991) *Managing Brand Equity*. Free Press, p. 15

AASB (1996) *Accounting for Goodwill*. AASB1013, Australian Accounting Standards Board

Aitken, M. (1990) A general theory of financial reporting: is it possible? *International Journal of Accounting*, **25**(4), 221–33

Anson, W. (1998) The million dollar domain name. *Managing Intellectual Property*, May, 40–43

Archer, S. (1994) *Responses to Discussion Paper Accounting for Goodwill and Intangible Assets*. Accounting Standards Board, pp. 15–25

Arnold, J., Egginton, D., Kirkham, L., Macve, R. and Peasnell, K. (1992) *Goodwill and Other Intangible Assets*. ICAEW Research Board, pp. 1–93

Arthur Andersen (1992) *The Valuation of Intangible Assets*. Economist Intelligence Unit, pp. 1–104

Arthur Andersen (1994) *Responses to Discussion Paper Accounting for Goodwill and Intangible Assets*. Accounting Standards Board, p. 34

ASB (1993) *Discussion Paper: Goodwill and Intangible Assets*. Accounting Standards Board, pp. 1–70

ASB (1994) *Acquisitions and Mergers*. FRS6, Accounting Standards Board, pp. 1–61

ASB (1995a) *Goodwill & Intangible* Assets. Working paper for discussion at public hearing, Accounting Standards Board, pp. 1–30

ASB (1995b) *Exposure Draft: Statement of Principles for Financial Reporting*, Accounting Standards Board, pp. 1–132

ASB (1995c) *Responses to the Working Paper on Goodwill & Intangible Assets*, Accounting Standards Board, pp. 1–359 plus late responses

ASB (1995x, y, z) *Responses to the Public Hearings on Goodwill & Intangible Assets* held 26–28 September. Accounting Standards Board (x = day 1, y = day 2, z = day 3)

ASB (1996) *Goodwill and Intangible Assets*. FRED12, Accounting Standards Board, pp. 1–7

ASB (1997) *Goodwill and Intangible Assets*. FRS10, Accounting Standards Board, pp. 1–77

ASB (1998) *Impairment of Fixed Assets and Goodwill*. FRS11, Accounting Standards Board, pp. 1–64

ASB (1999) *Revised Financial Reporting Exposure Draft: Statement of Principles for Financial Reporting*. Accounting Standards Board, pp. 1–108

ASB (2001) *Accounting Policies*. FRS18, Accounting Standards Board, pp. 1–64

ASC (1971) *Disclosure of Accounting Policies*. SSAP2, Accounting Standards Committee

ASC (1980) *Current Cost Accounting*. SSAP16, Accounting Standards Committee

ASC (1989a) *Accounting for Research and Development*. SSAP13, Accounting Standards Committee

ASC (1989b) *Accounting for Goodwill*. SSAP22, revised edition, Accounting Standards Committee, pp. 1–15

ASC (1990) *Accounting for Intangible Fixed Assets*. ED52, Accounting Standards Committee, p. 10

ASRB (1990) *Accounting for Business Combinations*. SSAP8, Institute of Chartered Accountants of New Zealand. *New Zealand Accounting Standards* 2001. New Zealand Accounting Standards Review Board, pp. 1–23

Bainbridge, D. (1994) *Intellectual Property*, 2nd edn. Pitman, p. 403

Barwise, P., Higson, C., Likierman, A. and Marsh, P. (1989) *Accounting for Brands*. ICAEW/LBS, pp. 1–84

Baxter, W. T. (1993) *Asset Values—Goodwill and Brand Names*. ACCA Occasional Research Report 14, Chartered Association of Certified Accountants, pp. 1–35

Beaver, W. H. (1981) *Financial Reporting: An Accounting Revolution*. Prentice Hall

Bennet, P. D. (1988) *Dictionary of Marketing Terms*. American Marketing Association

Brand Finance (2000) *Brand Finance Report*. Brand Finance plc, London

Bromley, D. W. (1967) Distributional implications of the extended economic zone: some policy and research issues in the fishery. *American Journal of Agricultural Economics*, **59**: 887–92

Brummet, R. L., Flamholtz, E. G. and Pyle, W. C. (1968) Human resource measurement—a challenge for accountants. *Accounting Review*, **43**, 217–24

Brummet, R. L., Flamholtz, E. G. and Pyle, W. C. (1969a) Human resource myopia. *Monthly Labour Review*, Jan, 29–30

Brummet, R. L., Flamholtz, E. G. and Pyle, W. C. (1969b) Human resource accounting: a tool to increase managerial effectiveness. *Management Accounting*, **51**, 20–25

Catlett, R. C. and Olson, N. O. (1968) Accounting for Goodwill, *AICPA Accounting Research Study 10*. AICPA, pp. 17–18

Chambers, R. J. (1966) *Accounting Evaluation and Economic Behavior*. Prentice Hall, p. 103

Chambers, R. J. (1991) Metrical and empirical laws in accounting. *Accounting Horizons*, **5**(4), 1–15

Chartered Institute of Marketing (1993) A view from the institute. *Marketing Business*, Feb, 20

Chauvin, K. W. and Hirschey, M. (1994) Goodwill, profitability and the market value of the firm. *Journal of Accounting and Public Policy*, **13**(2), 159–80

Checkland, A. (1988) Information systems and systems thinking: time to unite? *International Journal of Information Management*, **8**, 239–48

CICA (1974) Business combinations—section 1580. *Canadian Institute of Chartered Accountants Handbook*, Release 4, March 1999

Coopers & Lybrand (1994) *Responses to Discussion Paper Accounting for Goodwill and Intangible Assets*. Accounting Standards Board, pp. 106–8

Damant (1995) *Responses to Working Paper: Accounting for Goodwill and Intangible Assets*. Accounting Standards Board, p. 73

Davidson, J. H. (1999) Transforming the value of company reports through marketing measurement. *Journal of Marketing Management*, **15**, 757–77

Davies, M. J. and Davies, P. H. (1994) *Responses to Discussion Paper Accounting for Goodwill and Intangible Assets*. Accounting Standards Board, pp. 117–24

Dicksee, L. R. (1897) Goodwill and its treatment in accounts. *The Accountant*, Jan, 40–48

Dzinkowski, R. (2000) The measurement and management of intellectual capital. *Management Accounting*, Feb, 32–36

Edvinson, L. and Malone, M. (1997) *Intellectual capital: realising your company's true value by finding its hidden brainpower*. HarperCollins

Egginton, D. (1990) Towards some principles for intangible asset accounting. *Accounting and Business Research*, **20**(79), 193–205

Ernst & Young (1994) *Responses to Discussion Paper Accounting for Goodwill and Intangible Assets*. Accounting Standards Board, p. 126

Falk, H. and Gordon, L. A. (1977) Imperfect markets and the nature of goodwill. *Journal of Business Finance and Accounting*, April, 450

Farquhar, P. H. (1989) Managing brand equity. *Marketing Research*, **1**(3), 24–33

FASB (1970a) APB Opinion 16: Business Combinations, Financial Accounting Standards Board. *Original Pronouncements 1999/2000*, pp. 202–22

FASB (1970b) APB Opinion 17: Intangible Assets, Financial Accounting Standards Board. *Original Pronouncements 1999/2000*, pp. 223–29

FASB (1980) Qualitative characteristics of accounting information. *Statement of Financial Accounting Concepts 2*, Financial Accounting Standards Board

FASB (1984) Recognition and measurement in financial statements of business enterprises. *Statement of Financial Accounting Concepts 5*, Financial Accounting Standards Board

FASB (1985) Elements of financial statements. *Statement of Financial Accounting Concepts 6*, Financial Accounting Standards Board, pp. 1–93

FASB (2001) Business combinations. *Financial Accounting Standard 141*, Financial Accounting Standards Board

Friedman, A. and Lev, B. (1974) A surrogate for the firms investment in human resources. *Journal of Accounting Research*, **12**, 235–50

FRSB (1999) Exposure Draft 87: Accounting for Intangible Assets. Financial Reporting Standards Board, Institute of Chartered Accountants of New Zealand, *New Zealand Accounting Standards 2001*, pp. 1–38

Gambling, T. E. (1971) Towards a general theory of accounting. *International Journal of Accounting*, **7**(1), 1–13

Gambling, T. E. (1974) System dynamics approach to human resource accounting. *Accounting Review*, **49**, 538–46

Gerboth, D. L. (1987) The conceptual framework: not definitions, but professional values. *Accounting Horizons*, **1**(3), 1–8

Grinyer, J. R. (1994) *Responses to Discussion Paper Accounting for Goodwill and Intangible Assets*. Accounting Standards Board, pp. 155–62

Grinyer, J. R., Russell, A. and Walker, M. (1990) The rationale for accounting for goodwill. *British Accounting Review*, **22**(3), 223–35

Grinyer, J. R., Russell, A. and Walker, M. (1991) Managerial choices in the valuation of acquired goodwill in the UK. *Accounting and Business Research*, **22**(85), 51–55

Gu, F. and Lev, B. (2001) *Intangible assets—measurement, drivers, usefulness*, April, Baruch Lev's homepage www.stern.nyu.edu/blev

Haigh, D. (2000) Walking away from a $3bn brand. *Accountancy Age*, 14 September, pp. 22–23

Hamilton, M. B. (1987) The elements of the concept of ideology. *Political Studies*, **XXXV**(1), 18–38

Hart, S. and Murphy, J. (1998) *Brands: The New Wealth Creators*. Macmillan, p. 98

Heigh, D. (1997) Getting the best from brands. *Managing Intellectual Property*, May, 44–48

Higson, C. (1998) Goodwill. *British Accounting Review*, **30**, 141–58

Hines, R. (1988) Financial accounting: in communicating reality, we construct reality. *Accounting, Organisations and Society*, **13**(3), 251–61

Hines, R. D. (1991) The FASB's conceptual framework, financial accounting and the maintenance of the social world. *Accounting, Organisations and Society*, **16**(4), 313–31

Hodgson, A., Okunev, J. and Willett, R. (1993) Accounting for intangibles: a theoretical perspective. *Accounting and Business Research*, **23**(90), 138–50

Holmes, O. W. (1897) The path of the law. *Harvard Law Review*, 25 March, p. 466

Honoré, A. M. (1961) Ownership. In Guest, A. G. (ed.) *Oxford Essays in Jurisprudence*. Oxford University Press, Ch. 5

IASC (1989) *Framework for the preparation and presentation of accounting statements*, International Accounting Standards Committee, p. 9

IASC (1998) Business combinations, IAS22. *International Accounting Standards 2000*, International Accounting Standards Committee, pp. 541–86

Ijiri, Y. (1965) Axioms and structures of conventional accounting measurement. *Accounting Review*, Jan, 36–53

Jaggi, B. L. and Lau, H. S. (1974) Toward a model for human resource valuation. *Accounting Review*, **49**, 321–29

Jennings, R., Robinson, J., Thompson, R. B. and Duvall, L. (1996) The relation between accounting goodwill numbers and equity values. *Journal of Business Finance and Accounting*, **23**(4), 513–33

Johanson, U. (1999) Why the concept of human resource accounting does not work. *Personnel Review*, **28**(1/2), 91–107

Kaplan, R. S. and Norton, D. P. (1992) The balanced scorecard—measures that drive performance. *Harvard Business Review*, Jan/Feb, 71–79

Kennedy, S. (1998) Goodwill, brands and other intangibles. Conference documentation, 24 April, IBC Conferences, pp. 2–27

Koeppen, D. R. (1988) Using the FASB's conceptual framework: fitting the pieces together. *Accounting Horizons*, **2**(2), 18–26

Kotler, P. (1980) *Marketing Management*, 4th edn. Prentice Hall (10th edn, 1999)

KPMG (1994) *Responses to Discussion Paper Accounting for Goodwill and Intangible Assets*, Accounting Standards Board, p. 253

Laughlin, R. (1995) Methodological themes—empirical research in accounting: alternative approaches and a case for 'middle-range' thinking. *Accounting, Auditing and Accountability Journal*, **8**(1), 63–87

Lee, T. (1971) Goodwill—an example of will-o'-the-wisp accounting. *Accounting and Business Research*, Autumn, 318–28

Lee, T. (1993) Goodwill—further attempts to capture the will-o'-the-wisp: a review of an ICAEW research report. *Accounting and Business Research*, **24**(93), 79–81

Likert, R. and Pyle, W. C. (1971) Human resource accounting: a human organizational measurement approach. *Financial Analysts Journal*, **27**, 75–84

Llewellyn, S. (1994) Managing the boundary. *Accounting, Auditing and Accountability Journal*, **7**(4), 4–23

McCarthy, M. G. and Schneider, D. K. (1995) Market perception of goodwill: some empirical evidence. *Accounting and Business Research*, **26**(1), 69–81

Mainz, A. and Mullen, M. (1989) Putting a price on protected products. *Acquisitions Monthly*, April, 24–27

Marsden, D. and Littler, D. (1996) Evaluating alternative research paradigms: a market-orientated framework. *Journal of Marketing Management*, **12**, 645–55

Mattessich, R. (1964) *Accounting and Analytical Methods*. Irwin

Mautz, R. K. (1988) Monuments, mistakes and opportunities. *Accounting Horizons*. **2**(2), 123–28

Meyer, J. W. (1983) On the celebration of rationality: some comments on Boland and Pondy. *Accounting, Organisations and Society*, **8**(2/3), 235–40

Meyer-Rochow R. (1998) The application of passing off as a remedy against domain name piracy. *European Intellectual Property Review*, **11**, 405–9

Moore, D. C. (1991) Accounting on trial: the critical legal studies movement and its lessons for radical accounting. *Accounting, Organisations and Society*, **16**(8), 763–91

Morgan, G. (1980) Paradigms, metaphors and puzzle solving in organization theory. *Administrative Science Quarterly*, Cornell University, pp. 605–21

Murphy, J. (1990a) Brand valuation—not just an accounting issue. *ADMAP*, April, 36–41

Murphy, J. (ed.) (1990b) *Brand Valuation—Establishing a True and Fair View*. Hutchinson

Murray, A. D. (1997) A distinct lack of goodwill. *European Intellectual Property Review*, **7**, 345–50

Napier, C. and Power, M. (1992) Professional research, lobbying and intangibles: a review essay. *Accounting and Business Research*, **23**(89), 85–95

Nelson, R. H. (1953) The momentum theory of goodwill. *Accounting Review*, Oct, 494–97

OECD (1996) Measuring what people know. In *Human Capital Accounting for the Knowledge Economy*. OECD Publications

Oldroyd, D. (1994) Accounting and marketing: the juxtaposition within brands. *International Marketing Review*, **11**(2), 33–46

Pallot, J. (1990) The nature of public assets: a response to Mautz. *Accounting Horizons*, **4**(2), 79–85

Popper, K. R. (1962) *The Open Society and Its Enemies*, Vol. 2. Routledge & Kegan Paul, p. 19

Quah, D. T. (1997) Weightless economy packs a heavy punch. *Independent on Sunday*, 18 May, p. 4

Rose, D. (1998) UK sends a warning to cyber-pirates. *Managing Intellectual Property*, Sept, pp. 69–71

Russell, A., Grinyer, J. R., Walker, M. and Malton, P. A. (1989) *Accounting for goodwill*. Certified Research Report 13, Chartered Association of Certified Accountants, pp. 1–34

Sackmann, S. A., Flamholtz, E. G. and Bullen, M. L. (1989) Human resource accounting: a state of the art review. *Journal of Accounting Literature*, **8**, 235–64

Scarpello, V. and Theeke, H. A. (1989) Human resource accounting: a measured critique. *Journal of Accounting Literature*, **8**, 265–80

Schuetze, W. P. (1993) What is an asset? *Accounting Horizons*, **7**(3), 66–70

Sherer, M. J. (1991) Accounting for brands: a review essay. *British Accounting Review*, **23**(2), 179–82

Simmonds, A. (1994) *Touche Ross Responses to Discussion Paper Accounting for Goodwill and Intangible Assets*. Accounting Standards Board, pp. 423–66

Solomons, D. (1989) *Guidelines for Financial Reporting Standards*. Prepared for the Research Board of the Institute of Chartered Accountants in England and Wales

Sterling, R. R. (1970) *Theory of Measurement of Enterprise Income*. Kansas University Press

Stoy Hayward (1994) *Responses to Discussion Paper Accounting for Goodwill and Intangible Assets*. Accounting Standards Board, p. 412

Tearney, M. G. (1973) Accounting for goodwill: a realistic approach. *Journal of Accountancy*, July, 41–45

Tollington, T. (1998a) Separating the brand asset from the goodwill asset. *Journal of Product and Brand Management*, **7**(4), 291–304

Tollington, T. (1998b) What are assets anyway? Some practical realities. *Management Decision*, **36**(7), 448–55

Tollington, T. (1998c) Brands: the asset definition and recognition test. *Journal of Product and Brand Management*, **7**(3), 180–92

Tollington, T. (1999) The brand accounting sideshow. *Journal of Product and Brand Management*, **8**(3), 204–17

Tollington, T. (2001a) The separable nature of brand assets: the UK legal and accounting perspective. *European Intellectual Property Review*, **23**(1), 6–13

Tollington, T. (2001b) UK Brand asset recognition beyond 'transactions or events'. *Long Range Planning*, **34**(4), 463–87

Tracey, S. (1998) Winning the brand battle in the supermarket. *Managing Intellectual Property*, July/Aug, 17–20

Turner, G. (1996) Human resource accounting—whim or wisdom? *Journal of Human Resource Costing and Accounting*, **1**(1), 63–73

Van Mesdag M. (1993) Brands on the balance sheet, *Marketing Business*, Feb, 18–20

Vaughan, J. L. (1972) Give intangible assets useful life. *Harvard Business Review*, Sept/Oct, 127–32

Walsh, P. (1998) Securing trade dress protection in the UK: trade mark year book 1998. *A supplement to Managing Intellectual Property*, pp. 53–55

Weetman, P. (1989) Assets and liabilities: their definition and recognition. *ACCA Research Report* 14, Certified Accountant Publications, p. 34

Whittington, G. (1974) Asset valuation, income measurement and accounting income. *Accounting and Business Research*, Spring, 96–101

Willett, R. J. (1987) An axiomatic theory of accounting measurement. *Accounting and Business Research*, Spring, 155–71

Willett, R. J. (1988) An axiomatic theory of accounting measurement—part II. *Accounting and Business Research*, **19**(73), 79–91

Wines, G. and Ferguson, C. (1993) An empirical investigation of accounting methods of goodwill and identifiable assets: 1985–1989. *ABACUS*, **29**(1), 90–105

List of cases

Associated Newspapers plc v Insert Media Ltd (1990, 1 WLR 900–8)

Glaxo plc v Glaxowellcome Ltd (1996, FSR 388)

Harrods Ltd v Harrodian School Ltd (1996, RPC 697)

Harrods v UK Network Services Ltd (1997, 4 EIPR D-106)

Lego Systems Aktieselskab v Lego Lemelstrich Ltd (1983, FSR 641)

Marks & Spencer plc v One In A Million (28 November 1997, unreported)

Reckitt & Colman Products v Borden Inc. (1990, RPC 341)

Taittinger SA v Allbev Ltd (1993, FSR 641)

United Biscuits (UK) Ltd v Asda Stores Ltd (Chancery Division, 18 March 1997)

Index

RIT - WALLACE LIBRARY
CIRCULATING LIBRARY BOOKS

OVERDUE FINES AND FEES FOR <u>ALL</u> BORROWERS

*Recalled = $1/ day overdue (no grace period)
*Billed = $10.00/ item when returned 4 or more weeks overdue
*Lost Items = replacement cost+$10 fee
*All materials must be returned or renewed by the duedate.